P · O · C · K · E · T · S

WORLD
HISTORY

HITTITE
SOLDIER, C.1000 BC

BABYLONIAN
SOLDIER, C.1000 BC

ASSYRIAN
SOLDIER, C.1000 BC

LOUIS XIV OF FRANCE,
1638–1715

BE 2B BOMBER,
1914

GREAT WALL OF
CHINA, 221 BC

ALFRED JEWEL,
C.AD 890

P · O · C · K · E · T · S

WORLD HISTORY

Written by
PHILIP WILKINSON

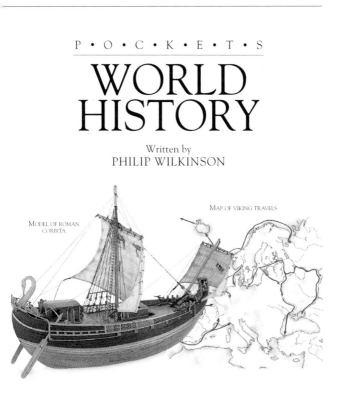

MAP OF VIKING TRAVELS

MODEL OF ROMAN
CORBITA

A DK PUBLISHING BOOK

Project editor	Claire Watts
Designer	Kate Eagar
Art editors	Carole Oliver
	Sarah Ponder
Senior editor	Hazel Egerton
Senior art editor	Jacquie Gulliver
Researcher	Robert Graham
Picture research	Sharon Southren
Production	Josie Alabaster
US editor	Constance M. Robinson
US consultant	Colleen Filler

First American edition, 1996
2 4 6 8 10 9 7 5 3 1

Published in the United States by DK Publishing, Inc.,
95 Madison Avenue, New York, New York 10016

Library of Congress Cataloging-in-Publication Data
Wilkinson, Philip. 1955–
    World history / by Philip Wilkinson. – 1st American ed.
    p. cm. – (DK pockets)
    Summary: Surveys the cultural, political, artistic, and scientific highlights of major civilizations
throughout history.
    ISBN 0-7894-0603-9
    1. World history–Juvenile literature. 2. Civilization–History–Juvenile literature.
    [1. World history. 2. Civilization–History.] I. Title. II. Series.
D21.W68 1996   95-43794
909–dc20   CIP
                                                                AC

Color reproduction by Colourscan, Singapore
Printed and bound in Italy by L.E.G.O.

CONTENTS

HOW TO USE THIS BOOK

These pages show you how to use *Pockets: World History*. The book is divided into six sections covering different historical periods or events, and there is a reference section at the end. Each new section begins with a contents page and one or more time charts.

HEADING AND INTRODUCTION
The heading describes the subject of a page. If a subject continues over more than one page, the same heading applies. Some pages are divided further by subheadings. The introduction follows, and provides an overview of the subject.

CHARTS
Some pages have helpful charts that give a clear summary of information, such as major events, key dates, characters, or inventions.

FACT BOXES
Many pages contain fact boxes, colored yellow. These boxes give at-a-glance information and provide extra facts about the subject.

Heading   Introduction   *Timeline*

Caption

THE HUNDRED YEARS WAR
WHEN EDWARD III (1312-77) was crowned King of England in 1327, he thought he also had a good claim to the French throne through his mother. In 1337, he declared war on France, beginning a conflict that was to last over a hundred years, until the final French victory in 1453.

Annotation

CHAIN MAIL
In the 14th century, soldiers wore shirts made of linked iron rings.

Feature box

ABBREVIATIONS
USED IN THIS BOOK

AD	Anno Domini
b.	born
BC	before Christ
c.	circa (around)
d.	died
MYA	million years ago
YA	years ago

FEATURE BOXES
Feature boxes supply extra information about a subject or cover an event that was taking place elsewhere at the same time.

CAPTIONS, LABELS, AND ANNOTATIONS
Each illustration has a caption, and many have labels, for extra clarity. Annotations in *italics* give details about the picture.

At the top of each text page, you will find a yellow timeline with a contrasting part. The dates at each end of the line refer to the section you are in. The part marked in a contrasting color refers to the period covered by the page you are on.

	3 MYA TO 5000 BC
	5000 BC TO AD 600
	600 TO 1400
	1400 TO 1750
	1750 TO 1900
	1900 TO 1990s

Chart *Fact box*

The Black Death

■ 1347. An epidemic swept across Europe. In four years, some 25 million people (about a quarter of the population) died of the Black Death, a combination of pneumonic and bubonic plague.

SPREAD OF THE PLAGUE
The Black Death was carried by fleas that lived on rats. The epidemic originated in Asia and rapidly spread westward. Only a few areas escaped the dreaded disease, including parts of Poland, Flanders, southwest France, and Milan.

Map *Subheading*

MAPS
Many pages contain maps. These may show where particular civilizations lived, or what areas they traveled to. The map on this page illustrates how the Black Death spread across Europe.

TIME CHARTS
At the beginning of each section, you will find illustrated time charts. You can use these to compare events that were happening at the same time. The symbol ➡ means that you will find more information about the entry on the page indicated.

REFERENCE SECTION, GLOSSARY, AND INDEX
At the back of the book, a reference section lists important world rulers, a glossary explains difficult words used in the book, and an index lists every subject in the book.

WHAT IS HISTORY?

FOR ALMOST AS LONG as people have been able to write, they have been writing about the past. Historians look at all sorts of different aspects of the past – rulers and governments, wars and battles, and the daily lives of ordinary people.

ANCIENT
EGYPTIAN
MUMMY

INVENTIONS
New inventions have changed the world. The wheel was one of the greatest transportation inventions. Stirrups allowed warriors to ride and fight at the same time.

STIRRUP,
C.AD 900

WHEEL,
C.3200 BC

WHY DID THEY DO THAT?
Many of the things people did in the past seem very odd today. Historians try to work out why people did certain things, for example, why the Egyptians made mummies.

FAMOUS HISTORIANS

NAME	DATE	INFORMATION
Herodotus	c.484 BC–c.425 BC	Greek "father of history"; wrote about the military and political history of the ancient world.
Bede	c.672–735	English historian who wrote a well-researched account of the English church and people.
Francesco Guicciardini	1483–1540	Italian historian who wrote eyewitness accounts of events that he had lived through.
Edward Gibbon	1737–1794	English historian who analyzed the patterns of events, especially the fall of the Roman Empire.
Fernand Braudel	1902–1985	French historian who began to look at economic factors and the lives of ordinary people.

Picture of the past

Historians study a range of evidence and interpret it to build up a picture of the past. A historian studying the life of a medieval knight would look at documents, buildings, and archaeological artifacts to gain a complete view of the subject.

MEN AT ARMS
This picture, copied from a drawing done at the time, shows that archers aimed their bows high.

WEAPONS OF WAR
Medieval arrowheads unearthed by archaeologists show that the arrows were sharp enough to pierce armor.

Castle contained accommodations for the lord and his family, and rooms for soldiers

Village occupied by tenant farmers

Curtain wall protects outer courtyard

DEFENSE
Castles were built so that they would be easy to defend. Animals and a vegetable garden provided food in case of siege.

CASTLE, 13TH CENTURY

HISTORICAL EVIDENCE

EVERYTHING, FROM AN old document to a building, a priceless jewel to a piece of litter, can provide clues about the past. This evidence can show us where people lived, what they did, and what was important to them. Interpreting evidence is the most fascinating part of the historian's job.

Inscription

ALFRED
JEWEL, C.890

LUXURY ARTIFACTS
Richly decorated artifacts provide evidence about their period, such as the clothes people wore, the skill of craft workers, and people's wealth.

VIKING COMB,
800s

Carved from
elk antler

EVERYDAY ARTIFACTS
Simple items like this Viking comb can be very revealing. The discoveries of many combs show that appearance and health were important to the Vikings.

BUILDINGS
Architecture can provide fascinating historical evidence. The Colosseum tells us much about Roman life. The seats of different ranks of Roman society, the cages of the animals, and the cells of the gladiators can all be seen among the ruins.

COLOSSEUM, ROME, AD 80

HISTORICAL DOCUMENTS

WRITTEN DOCUMENTS
All kinds of books and papers are useful to historians, from actual accounts of past events to texts that show the interests and beliefs of people in the past.

Text of a prayer

LOTUS SUTRA, C.1000

CARVED WORDS
Texts are not always written in the form of books or scrolls. Over the years, people have used bone, silk, copper, stone, and wood to write on.

RUNIC INSCRIPTION, GREENLAND, C.1000

RECORDS WITHOUT WRITING
Even cultures that never developed writing invented their own ways of keeping records.

INCA QUIPU, C.1480

Knots record numbers of items

MAPS
Old maps can show how much of the world was known to their makers, and which places were considered important.

GLOBE, C.1600

MAKING TODAY'S HISTORY
Modern historians may use newspapers as an important source. They read many accounts of an event to try to get an overview of different opinions.

MODERN NEWSPAPERS

ARCHAEOLOGY

ARCHAEOLOGISTS study
remains from the past –
everything from fragments of
pottery to human skeletons,
from the foundations of old
buildings to bits of industrial
machinery. Modern
archaeologists use scientific
methods to analyze their
finds and work out what life
was like in the past.

HUMAN REMAINS
Human bones, like this skull from
the Roman city of Herculaneum,
can tell archaeologists how tall
people were, what diseases they
suffered from, and even what they
usually ate.

EQUIPMENT AND TECHNIQUES

NAME	TOOL	INFORMATION
Trowel		Many archaeologists spend much of their time digging. Soil must be removed slowly and carefully, so as not to destroy any evidence.
Find bag		Every find is carefully recorded, numbered, bagged, and labeled. Recording is the most important of the archaeologist's jobs. Historians will be able to make full use of the finds only if the site and evidence are properly recorded.
Calipers		Each find must be measured. With delicate and irregular items, it can sometimes be difficult to use a tape measure, so calipers are used to gauge the exact size of the object.
Pole		Scale poles are placed next to objects that are photographed, so that it is easy to see how large the item is.

INTERPRETING THE LANDSCAPE

High sun

No shadows

NOON
Remains of old buildings may appear as bumps on the surface. These are difficult to see when the sun is high in the sky.

Low sun

Shadows form

SUNSET OR DAWN
When the sun is low, the bumps can be seen more clearly, allowing archaeologists to work out what is underground.

Building stones stunt crops

Here, crops grow quickly

CROP GROWTH
Underground remains such as ditches or stones can affect crops. These differences can be seen easily from the air.

EXCAVATION
Archaeologists carefully select a spot on an interesting site for an excavation or "dig." When the topsoil has been removed, they gradually take away layers of soil, recording everything they find.

Removing soil from a pot using a small brush

An artist records finds

Scraping around a pot with a trowel

Area is divided into a grid, so that the position of finds can be recorded accurately

3 MYA TO 5000 BC

TIME CHART

	3 MYA	500,000 YA	50,000 BC
EVENTS	**3 MYA** *Australopithecus*, the first hominid to walk upright, appears in southern and eastern Africa ➔ 20 **2 MYA** *Homo habilis*, a tool-making hominid, appears in Africa **1.7 MYA** *Homo erectus* appears in eastern Africa ➔ 20 **1 MYA** *Homo erectus* has spread to eastern Asia and Java MAMMOTH HUNT, 13,000 BC	**120,000 YA** Neanderthal people (*Homo sapiens neanderthalis*) appear in Europe and western Asia **100,000 YA** Modern humans (*Homo sapiens sapiens*) appear in Africa ➔ 20	**50,000 BC** Neanderthals present in western Europe, western Asia, and Uzbekistan **40,000 BC** Colonization of Australia by early *Homo sapiens sapiens* **40,000 BC** Cro-Magnon man (early *Homo sapiens sapiens*) reaches Europe from Africa **30,000 YA** Beginning of last ice age ➔ 21 **30,000 BC** Neanderthals die out **25,000 BC** Start of coldest period of last ice age
ARTS & ARCHITECTURE		**450,000 YA** Simple stone windbreaks used for shelter, France **380,000 YA** Earliest known artificial shelter, France	**50,000 BC** Neanderthals engrave patterns on stone to make simple art objects **24,000 BC** Earliest known rock paintings, Africa **23,000 BC** Earliest known clay figures, Europe
SCIENCE & INVENTION	**3 MYA** Possible use of simple pebble tools ➔ 20, 21 **2 MYA** Simple stone tools used to make other tools **1.7 MYA** Hand ax first made; used as a general-purpose tool ➔ 20, 21	**460,000 YA** Earliest known use of fire, China **100,000 YA** Earliest known burials **100,000 YA** Specialized stone tools ➔ 21	**25,000 BC** Various methods of cooking food develop **24,000 BC** Earliest known cremation, Australia FOOD WRAPPED IN LEAVES, 25,000 BC

20,000 BC	12,000 BC	8000 BC
18,000 BC Coldest point of last ice age	FARMING, WESTERN ASIA 9000 BC	
18,000 BC Settlement of Zaire, central Africa	**11,000 BC** Colonization of South America begins with the arrival of people in Chile	
17,000 BC Wild cereal gathering, western Asia ➡ 22	**10,000 BC** End of last ice age	
13,000 BC Colonization of North America begins with the crossing of the land bridge between Asia and Alaska	**9000 BC** Extinction of mammoth, perhaps due to overhunting	**8000 BC** Settlement of Jericho ➡ 24, 25
13,000 BC Ice-age people hunt woolly mammoths ➡ 21	**9000 BC** Farming begins, western Asia ➡ 22, 23	**6000 BC** Cattle domesticated, Sahara
13,000 BC Rising sea levels submerge lowlands as the ice begins to thaw	**9000 BC** First people reach tip of South America	**6000 BC** New Guinea and Tasmania are cut off from Australia as sea level rises
20,000 BC–10,000 BC Cave paintings produced, France and Spain	MAMMOTH-BONE HUT, 16,000 BC	**8000 BC** First large buildings of sun-dried bricks, western Asia
16,000 BC Mammoth-bone huts built, Europe		**c.7000 BC** Animal carvings made in bone, antler, and amber, Denmark and southern Sweden
18,000 BC Bone needles used, Australia	**11,000 BC** Tools made from obsidian, a black volcanic glass, Greece	**7500 BC** Earliest known cemetery, North America
	10,500 BC First pottery, Japan ➡ 25	**7000 BC** Early metal-working using raw copper and gold nuggets beaten into shape, western Asia
BONE NEEDLES, 18,000 BC	**9000 BC** First sun-dried mud bricks, western Asia	**7000 BC** Stone spade first used, China

EARLY PEOPLE

FOSSIL REMAINS SHOW that two million years ago several species of humanlike creatures (hominids) existed at the same time. Gradually, more intelligent and skillful species of hominids developed, and older species died out. Then, about 100,000 years ago, the first true humans (*Homo sapiens sapiens*) appeared.

Early female statues are always faceless

IVORY
VENUS,
FRANCE,
C.25,000 YA

BRAINS AND SKULLS

AUSTRALOPITHECUS
These creatures lived in Africa and were probably the first primates to walk upright. They had small brains, long arms, and large, powerful jaws with strong teeth.

3 MYA

HOMO ERECTUS
This species had larger skulls than previous hominids. They invented the hand ax, a sharp cutting or chopping tool, and learned to make fire.

1.7 MYA

HOMO SAPIENS SAPIENS
Our own ancestors were skillful tool-makers and hunter-gatherers. By about 35,000 years ago, they had spread all over Europe and reached Australia.

100,000 YA

THE FIRST ART
Early people decorated caves with paintings of bison, wild cattle, and horses. They also produced small statuettes, often of female figures.

The Ice Age

The last Ice Age occurred between 30,000 BC and 10,000 BC. Much of the world was colder, the sea level was lower, and North Africa had a damp climate. People adapted well to these conditions. When they killed an animal, they used every part. The flesh was eaten, the skins made into clothes, and the bones used for tools.

Covered pit to trap the mammoth

Stones were used to stun the mammoth

Wooden spear with flint blade

Coat made from animal skins

MAMMOTH HUNT

FOOD SUPPLY

In spring, summer, and autumn, people gathered plant foods to eat, but in winter, they relied on meat. They usually hunted in groups, and then shared the kill among the hunters.

TECHNOLOGY	ITEM	FUNCTION	FOUND
BOW AND ARROWS		Comb	Mesopotamia
FLINT SCRAPER *Sharp stone arrowhead*		Needle	Eastern Mediterranean
HAND AX		Harpoon	Europe
		Fishhook	Europe
		Beads	Eastern Mediterranean

Bows and arrows appeared in Africa between 30,000 and 15,000 BC. In Europe and Asia, spears and harpoons were used. As well as the hand ax, a range of more specialized tools was also produced.

SETTLERS AND FARMERS

AROUND 11,000 BC, the ice caps were retreating northward, bringing about climate changes and making the land more fertile. People in some parts of the world began to give up their wandering hunter-gatherer lifestyle and settle down. By 9000 BC, people had learned to plant and harvest cereal crops and to domesticate animals.

NATUFIAN SETTLEMENT

SETTLING DOWN

The Natufian people of Palestine were one of the first groups to live in permanent settlements. Some lived in caves; others built huts of mud, reeds, and lumber. The first Natufians gathered wild grain and stored it in their huts.

CROP CULTIVATION

Wild wheat, such as emmer and einkorn, is difficult to harvest because the ripe seed heads shatter. Early farmers combined existing varieties to develop better types of wheat.

Seed head easier to harvest

Small seeds

Wild emmer has small seeds

Domestic emmer has large seeds

Ripe seed head shatters

DOMESTIC EMMER

WILD EMMER

DOMESTIC EINKORN

WILD EINKORN

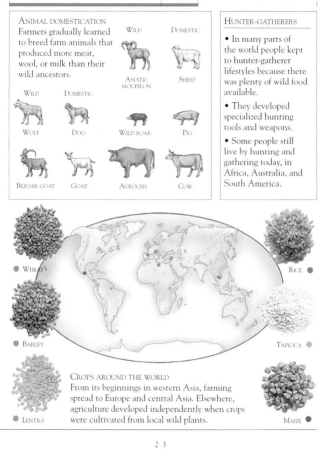

ANIMAL DOMESTICATION

Farmers gradually learned to breed farm animals that produced more meat, wool, or milk than their wild ancestors.

WILD   DOMESTIC

ASIATIC MOUFFLON   SHEEP

WILD   DOMESTIC

WOLF   DOG   WILD BOAR   PIG

BEZOAR GOAT   GOAT   AUROCHS   COW

HUNTER-GATHERERS

• In many parts of the world people kept to hunter-gatherer lifestyles because there was plenty of wild food available.

• They developed specialized hunting tools and weapons.

• Some people still live by hunting and gathering today, in Africa, Australia, and South America.

WHEAT   RICE ●

BARLEY   TAPIOCA ●

CROPS AROUND THE WORLD

From its beginnings in western Asia, farming spread to Europe and central Asia. Elsewhere, agriculture developed independently when crops were cultivated from local wild plants.

LENTILS   MAIZE ●

TOWNS AND TRADE

AS PEOPLE BEGAN to settle in groups, they found that they could specialize – some people farmed, while others made tools and pots. Villages began to produce more food and goods than they needed for themselves. They traded this surplus with other villages. The most successful trading communities grew into the first towns.

ÇATAL HÜYÜK, TURKEY
By about 6000 BC, 5,000 people lived in the town of Çatal Hüyük. The mud-brick houses were crowded together side by side with no streets. The town's inhabitants worked at home, making tools, weapons, and pottery. These were traded with people in the surrounding area for food, raw materials, and other goods.

Ladders connect roofs at different levels

Shrine with bull's horns on wall

Trap-door entrance

Wooden framework supports mud bricks

No streets between houses

EARLY TOWNS

TOWN	AREA	DATE	MAIN CRAFT
Jericho	Eastern Mediterranean	8000 BC	Pottery
Çatal Hüyük	Turkey	7000 BC	Pottery and obsidian tools
Jarmo	Iraq	7000 BC	Textiles
Khirokitia	Cyprus	6000 BC	Stone and wood items
Ugarit	Eastern Mediterranean	6000 BC	Textiles

IDEAS AND INNOVATIONS

DECORATED POT,
GERMANY, C.6000 BC

POTTERY
The art of pottery was first developed in Japan
in about 10,500 BC. Pots were usually made by
coiling a snakelike length of clay in a spiral, and
then smoothing down the surface.

SPINNING
Wool was twisted into a
strong thread using a
wooden spindle. This could
be woven to make warm cloth.

Wooden spindle

Raw wool

METAL-WORKING
The first metals were found
as pure lumps that could be beaten into shape.
By 6500 BC, people had discovered how to
extract metals from rocks.

*Casting, or
pouring molten
metal into a
mold*

MARKS OF OWNERSHIP
People in the early towns used clay stamps to
mark personal property and trade goods. The
seal was pushed into wet clay, which made a
permanent mark when the clay hardened.

*Indented
pattern*

STAMP SEALS,
IRAN, C.6000 BC

FIRST RELIGION
Early towns were often religious centers. The
people of Jericho decorated human skulls for
use in their religious rituals.

PLASTERED
SKULL,
JERICHO,
C.8000 BC

BREAD-MAKING
Grain was ground on a stone quern
to make flour. This was then mixed
with water, and baked in a dome-
shaped clay oven to make unleavened
(yeastless) bread. Once the dough was inside the oven, the
entrance was blocked up with clay to keep in the heat.

STONE
QUERN

5000 BC TO AD 600

TIME CHART

	5000 BC	4000 BC	3000 BC
EVENTS	**5000 BC** Corn first cultivated, Mexico **5000 BC** First cities are founded in Mesopotamia, western Asia ➡ 32, 33 **5000 BC** First settlements in Anahuac, Mexico **5000 BC** Rice first cultivated, China **4500 BC** Farming begins around River Ganges, India **4400 BC** Horses domesticated, Russia	ANIMALS DOMESTICATED, SAHARA, 4000 BC **4000 BC** Farming communities begin to domesticate animals, Sahara **3500 BC** City of Ur founded, Mesopotamia ➡ 32 **3500 BC** Earliest Chinese city, Liang-ch'eng chen, founded **c.3100 BC** Menes unites Upper and Lower Egypt	**3000 BC** Bronze age begins, Crete **2750 BC** Gilgamesh becomes King of Sumer **2686 BC–2182 BC** Old Kingdom period, Egypt **2500 BC** Sahara region begins to dry out **2330 BC** Sargon of Akkad (d.2275) dominates Sumer ➡ 33 **2300 BC** Beginning of Indus Valley civilization, Pakistan ➡ 33 **2133 BC–1786 BC** Middle Kingdom period, Egypt
ARTS & ARCHITECTURE	**5000 BC** First ziggurats built, Sumer ➡ 32 **4500 BC** Cave art flourishes, northern Africa **4500 BC** First megalithic tombs built, Britain and Portugal **4500 BC** Passage graves built, France	**4000 BC** Pyramid temples, Peru STONEHENGE, 2800 BC	**2800 BC** Building starts on Stonehenge, England **c.2646 BC** Building of Pyramid of Zoser, Egypt ➡ 34 **c.2590 BC** Building of Pyramid of Khufu, Egypt ➡ 34
SCIENCE & INVENTION	**5000 BC** Copper first used, Mesopotamia **5000 BC** Irrigation systems used, Mesopotamia SOWING RICE, CHINA, 5000 BC	**3500 BC** Plow and wheel used, Mesopotamia ➡ 33 **3500 BC** Sailing boats used on the Nile, Egypt ➡ 35 **3250 BC** Development of cuneiform, Mesopotamia ➡ 33	**3000 BC** Day divided into 24 hours, Babylon **3000 BC** Development of hieroglyphic script, Egypt ➡ 35 **2500 BC** Standard weights first used, Mesopotamia

2000 BC	1550 BC	1100 BC
2000 BC End of Sumerian power in Mesopotamia	**c.1500 BC** Collapse of Minoan civilization	**1100 BC** Rise of Phoenician civilization, eastern Mediterranean ➡ 36, 37
c.1790 BC Hammurabi (1792 BC–1750 BC) becomes King of Babylon ➡ 38	**1300 BC** Rise of Olmec civilization, Mexico	**c.970 BC** Solomon becomes King of Israel
1595 BC Hittites sack Babylon	**1279 BC** Rameses II (1290 BC–1213 BC) becomes pharaoh of Egypt ➡ 34	**900 BC** State of Sparta founded, Greece
1567 BC–1085 BC New Kingdom, Egypt	**1218 BC** Egypt and Eastern Mediterranean invaded by Sea Peoples from the Aegean	**814 BC** City of Carthage founded, North Africa
HAMMURABI	**1200 BC** Collapse of Hittite empire	**800 BC** Etruscan people establish city-states, western Italy ➡ 36, 37
	1200 BC Greeks destroy city of Troy after ten-year war	**776 BC** First Olympic Games held, Greece
	1200 BC Jews settle in Palestine	**753 BC** Rome founded
	1120 BC Mycenae destroyed	**604 BC** Nebuchadnezzar II (d.562 BC) becomes King of Babylon ➡ 39
2000 BC Minoan palaces built, Crete ➡ 36, 37	**1200 BC** Enamel used to decorate mummy cases	**973 BC** Solomon orders building of temple of Jerusalem
1600 BC Mycenaean citadels built, Greece ➡ 37		**800 BC–700 BC** Homer writes the *Odyssey* and the *Iliad*
	MINOAN PALACE, 2000 BC	**605–562 BC** Hanging gardens constructed, Babylon ➡ 39
2000 BC Chariot first used, Mesopotamia ➡ 38, 39	**1500 BC** Silk fabric first made, China	**620 BC** Coins first used, Asia
1900 BC Iron smelting, Mesopotamia	**1450 BC** First shadow clocks, Egypt	
1700 BC Early alphabetic script developed, Phoenicia	MESOPOTAMIAN CHARIOT 2000 BC	

TIME CHART

	600 BC	400 BC	200 BC
EVENTS	**563 BC–483 BC** Life of Buddha ➡ 43 **557 BC** Cyrus (d.529 BC) becomes King of Persia, and founds Persian Empire **551 BC–479 BC** Life of Confucius **510 BC** Roman Republic founded **500 BC** Beginning of iron-working Nok culture, Nigeria **490 BC** Battle of Marathon, Greece ➡ 41 **431 BC–404 BC** Peloponnesian Wars, Greece ➡ 41	**334 BC–326 BC** Alexander the Great (356 BC–323 BC) conquers much of Asia ➡ 41 **322 BC** Chandragupta Maurya founds Mauryan Empire, India ➡ 42 **264 BC–146 BC** Punic Wars between Rome and Carthage **221 BC** Unification of China ➡ 44 **216 BC** Roman army defeated by Hannibal (247 BC–183 BC) at Cannae	**147 BC–6 BC** Greece comes under Roman rule **49 BC** Julius Caesar (100 BC–44 BC) invades Gaul **46 BC** Caesar becomes Roman Dictator ➡ 47 **30 BC** Cleopatra (b.69 BC), ruler of Egypt, commits suicide **27 BC** Augustus (63 BC–AD 14) becomes first Roman Emperor ➡ 46 **c.4 BC–AD 30** Life of Jesus Christ ➡ 48 ROMAN SOLDIERS, 264 BC
ARTS & ARCHITECTURE	**600 BC** Temple of the Sun built, Meroë, Sudan **560 BC** Lao-Tzu (c.604 BC–c.531 BC) writes his philosophical work, *Tao Te Ching*, China **460 BC** Start of golden age of art and architecture, Greece	**290 BC** Foundation of library, Alexandria, Egypt **285 BC** Earliest known lighthouse, Pharos, Egypt **221 BC** Building starts on Great Wall of China ➡ 44	**100 BC** Terra-cotta art flourishes, India **30–19 BC** Virgil (70–19) writes the *Aeneid* GREAT WALL OF CHINA, 221 BC
SCIENCE & INVENTION	**550 BC** Maps first used by travelers **500 BC** Greeks develop oar-powered warship **500 BC** Persians begin to build road network **450 BC** Abacus used, Mediterranean	**400 BC** Hippocrates (460 BC–377 BC) sets up medical school, Greece **300 BC** Water clock invented, Egypt **230 BC** Earliest known metal springs, Alexandria, Egypt	**100 BC** Glass-blowing invented, Syria **100 BC** Stirrups first used, India **85 BC** Water-powered mill used for grinding grain, Greece

AD 1	AD 300	AD 400
AD 1 Beginning of Moche civilization, Peru	**212** Roman citizenship extended to all free-born people in the empire	**400s** Christianity becomes widespread in Axum Empire, northeast Africa ➡ 48
AD 43 Romans invade Britain	**220** End of Han dynasty, China ➡ 45	**410** Visigoths sack Rome
AD 50 Kingdom of Axum begins to expand, Ethiopia	**235–84** Period of civil war in Roman Empire	**445** Attila the Hun (406–453) attacks western Europe
AD 50 Buddhism reaches China ➡ 43	**284–305** Emperor Diocletian (245–313) restores order to Rome ➡ 47	**500** Hopewell culture at its peak, North America ➡ 51
AD 60–61 Rebellion of Boudicca (d.AD 61) against Romans in Britain	**311** Constantine (280–337) proclaimed Roman Emperor ➡ 48	**527** Justinian I (483–565) becomes Byzantine Emperor ➡ 49
AD 79 Eruption of Vesuvius destroys Pompeii, Italy	**360s** First invasion of Europe by Huns from Asia	**550** Buddhism introduced to Japan ➡ 43
AD 193 Septimius Severus (146–211) becomes Roman Emperor	**330** Foundation of Constantinople ➡ 49	**570–632** Life of Muhammad ➡ 58
AD 50 Nazca culture flourishes in Peru; Nazca people create vast lines and patterns in the desert	**397–401** St. Augustine (354–430) writes his *Confessions*	**537** Church of Hagia Sophia completed, Constantinople ➡ 49
AD 80 Colosseum opened, Rome		
AD 122–138 Hadrian's Wall built, Britain	HAGIA SOPHIA, AD 537	
AD 50 Horseshoe first used, Italy	**200** Cast iron invented, China	**500** Indian mathematicians introduce the zero
AD 100 Concrete used for building, Rome		**500** Stencil used for text, China and Japan
AD 105 Paper invented, China ➡ 44	PAPER, CHINA, AD 105	**599** Chess invented, India

THE FIRST CITIES

THE EARLIEST CITIES grew up in Mesopotamia, the
area between the Tigris and Euphrates rivers.
The land was fertile, so people grew grain and raised
animals. The Sumerians (the people of Mesopotamia)
traded grain with nearby areas, getting metals and
tools in return. Different cities dominated the region
at different times, but they all had a similar culture.

TEMPLES
The Sumerians had an organized religion
with many different gods. Each city had a
ziggurat (temple) consisting of a series of
platforms with stairs. The ziggurat at Ur,
built in about 2100 BC, was dedicated to the
moon god Nanna, who was the city's local
god. The priests made offerings to the
god every day.

SUMERIAN CITIES

Mari •
SUMERIAN
CIVILIZATION
Sippar •
Tigris
Euphrates
• Uruk
Ur • • Eridu

Sanctuary

*Processional
stairway*

Mud-brick
walls

Walls
decorated
with niches

ZIGGURAT, UR, 2100 BC

CUNEIFORM

The first picture-writing gradually developed into the cuneiform script used by the Sumerians. They used a reed to make marks in damp clay.

Record of foundation of building

FOUNDATION STONE, UR, c.2300 BC

PICTURE-WRITING, 3100 BC					
MEANING	Star	Stream	Barley	Bull's head	Bowl
CUNEIFORM, 2400 BC					
CUNEIFORM, 700 BC					
MEANING OF CUNEIFORM	God, sky	Water, seed	Barley	Ox	Food, bread

KINGS

Each city was ruled by a king with a team of priests. In c.2330 BC, Sargon II, King of Akkad, brought the whole of Mesopotamia under his rule.

Kings often had elaborate hairstyles

Cast bronze

Curled beard

SARGON II OF AKKAD

INVENTIONS

As well as the first writing system, the Sumerians invented the plow to improve agriculture, and the wheel to improve transportation.

WRITING   PLOW   WHEEL

BULL SEAL

IMPRESSION

INDUS VALLEY CIVILIZATION

Cities were also built near the Indus river between 2300 BC and 1750 BC. Indus Valley people used seals to show ownership of property.

ANCIENT EGYPT

THE CIVILIZATION OF ancient Egypt flourished for more than 3,000 years along the banks of the Nile. The country was ruled by pharaohs (kings) who had absolute power and were thought to become gods when they died. The Egyptians traded with other parts of Africa, Asia, and the Mediterranean.

FAMOUS PHARAOHS
• Zoser (c.2630 BC– 2611 BC) built the first pyramid, the Step Pyramid at Saqqara.
• Hatshepsut (c.1473 BC–1458 BC) was the world's first recorded female ruler.
• Rameses II (1290 BC–1213 BC) built new temples and conquered new territory.

King's burial chamber

Core of limestone

Mortuary temple

Small pyramid for one of Khufu's wives

Causeway

Funerary boat

GREAT PYRAMID OF KHUFU, GIZA

PYRAMIDS
Early pharaohs were buried in pyramids with all the possessions that the Egyptians thought they would need in the afterlife. Thousands of people worked on the Great Pyramid, which took over 20 years to build.

STEP PYRAMID, c.2646 BC   BENT PYRAMID, c.2600 BC   GREAT PYRAMID, c.2590 BC

Lavish
decoration

MUMMIES

Egyptians were mummified after death. Their inner organs were removed and placed in containers called canopic jars. Then the body was preserved with the chemical natron, wrapped in bandages, and placed in a papier-mâché coffin.

EAGLE	REED
SHUTTER	CHICK
SNAIL	OWL
DOUBLE REED	ARM

EGYPTIAN HIEROGLYPHS

The Egyptians developed their own system of writing. They wrote using hieroglyphs – simplified pictures that could represent sounds or actual objects. Scribes later developed two other scripts, hieratic and demotic, which were much simpler and quicker to write.

THE NILE RIVER

The Nile provided Egypt's main highway, along which everything from food to stone for the pyramids was carried. The Nile's yearly flooding also made the land fertile.

Wooden mast

Square sail

MODEL OF EGYPTIAN SAILING BOAT

Ropes supporting mast

Hull of cedar wood

Steering oar

MEDITERRANEAN POWERS

A GROUP OF PEOPLES dominated the Mediterranean
in the second millennium BC. The Minoans,
Mycenaeans, Phoenicians, and Etruscans lived in
groups of city-states, and they all used trade to extend
their influence. Each of these peoples had a typical
style of arts and crafts, so modern archaeologists have
been able to track their traders through objects found
in different places around the Mediterranean.

THE ETRUSCANS
The Etruscans
founded city-states in
Italy in about 800 BC.
They were renowned
for their art and
architecture. Little is
known about the
Etruscans'
history,
because their script has
not yet been
deciphered, but they
were conquered by the
Romans in the third
century BC.

Fine bronze and
pottery figures were
left in tombs

BRONZE WARRIOR,
C.800 BC

THE MINOANS
These people lived
on the island of
Crete. They traded
grain, wine, and oil
and used the wealth
they accumulated to
build a series of huge
palaces at Knossos, Mallia, Phaistos,
and Zakro. Beautiful palace wall-
paintings include scenes of people
leaping over the horns of running
bulls. No one knows why the
Minoans did this, but it may have
been part of a religious ritual.

STORAGE JAR,
KNOSSOS,
C.1500 BC

PAINTING OF BULL-LEAPING, KNOSSOS, C.1500 BC

- ● MINOANS, 2000 BC–1400 BC
- ● MYCENAEANS, 1600 BC–1200 BC
- ● ETRUSCANS, 800 BC–300 BC
- ● PHOENICIANS, 900 BC–600 BC

MEDITERRANEAN
CIVILIZATIONS

THE PHOENICIANS
Accomplished sailors,
the Phoenicians
traveled all over the
Mediterranean, trading
and founding cities as far
away as Spain and North
Africa. They made beautiful
glassware and sculptures, which
they sold to buy raw materials and
slaves. The Phoenicians also
developed a way of
dyeing cloth
purple using
murex shells.

MUREX
SHELL

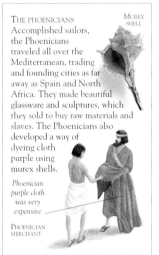

*Phoenician
purple cloth
was very
expensive*

PHOENICIAN
MERCHANT

THE MYCENAEANS
The Mycenaeans dominated
southern Greece and the Aegean
Sea, and took over Crete when the
Minoan civilization fell. They built
towns with strong walls and small
palaces for their kings.

FUNERARY
MASK OF
MYCENAEAN
KING, C.1550 BC

*Beaten
gold*

WESTERN ASIA

THE CITY-STATES OF western Asia gradually expanded into empires. The Assyrians, Hittites, and Babylonians formed large armies to conquer their neighbors. The peoples who were defeated had to send their conquerors tributes of goods and money, which financed the building of large cities such as Babylon.

HAMMURABI'S LAWS

Hammurabi, King of Babylon (1792 BC–1750 BC) established a code of 282 laws. These laws included:

• If a man robbed another, the robber was put to death.

• If a son hit his father, his hand was cut off.

• If a man put out the eye of another, his eye was put out, too.

SOLDIERS OF WESTERN ASIA

ASSYRIAN SOLDIER
Clad in their armor of metal scales, Assyrian soldiers were feared all over western Asia.

HITTITE SOLDIER
The Hittites were skilled with all weapons: bows and arrows, battle-axes, swords, and spears.

BABYLONIAN SOLDIER
Some Babylonian soldiers fought on foot, while others shot arrows from chariots.

Spear · *Pointed helmet*
Helmet with cheek and neck flaps
Spear
Scale armor
Sleeveless leather shirt
Round shield
Kilt
Kilt over scale armor

Chariots were small and light for maximum speed

HITTITE CHARIOTS

The Hittites used the chariot as a type of weapon. They drove through enemy lines at full speed, breaking up the ranks and causing chaos. Foot soldiers followed, picking off the weakened enemy.

THE CITY OF BABYLON

In 605 BC, when King Nebuchadnezzar II (d.562 BC) ruled Babylon, he expanded the empire and rebuilt the city. He created the famous hanging gardens, and added a large new gate and an avenue called the Sacred Way leading to the palace and the temple.

Temple to the god Marduk

Mud-brick houses

Palace with five courtyards

Hanging gardens with terraces of plants

Priest carrying lotus flower

ASSYRIAN ART

The Assyrians decorated their palaces with huge carved stone reliefs of kings and gods. They also carved tiny ivory reliefs.

Ishtar Gate

THE SACRED WAY, BABYLON, C.600 BC

ANCIENT GREECE

ANCIENT GREECE was not one country, but a series of city-states, each controlling lands in the surrounding area. The most powerful city-states were Athens and Sparta.

VOTING DISCS

DEMOCRACY
Decisions on how Athens was run were taken by a vote of male citizens. There was no vote for women or slaves.

GREEK VASES
The work of ancient Greek painters is preserved on many vases. Stories from Greek myths, animals, and scenes from daily life were popular subjects. This vase shows a scene from a symposium (banquet).

Guest

Kylix (drinking cup)

Musician

RED FIGURE VASE, 5TH CENTURY BC

GREEK GODS
The Greeks worshipped many gods, who were believed to live on Mount Olympus in northern Greece. Many Greek myths and plays told stories about the gods.

DEMETER, GODDESS OF FARMING

ZEUS, KING OF THE GODS

FAMOUS PHILOSOPHERS		
NAME	DATES	INTEREST
Socrates	469 BC–399 BC	Studied the principles that govern human life.
Plato	c.427 BC–347 BC	Wrote dialogues featuring his master, Socrates.
Aristotle	384 BC–322 BC	Concentrated on how the world works.

COLUMNS
These columns are typical of the three styles of Greek architecture.

DORIC   IONIC   CORINTHIAN

GREEK WARS
Challenges arose from various sources.

• The Greeks defeated Persian invaders at Marathon (490 BC) and Salamis (480 BC).

• In the Peloponnesian Wars (431 BC–404 BC), Sparta challenged and defeated Athens.

ARCHITECTURE
Greek cities had beautiful temples, theaters, and other public buildings. Some of the finest were built on the Acropolis, the hill overlooking the city of Athens.

Parthenon
(temple of Athena)

Propylea
(entrance to the Acropolis)

Theater of Dionysus

Sanctuary of Asclepius

THE ACROPOLIS, ATHENS

EMPIRE OF ALEXANDER THE GREAT, 323 BC

MACEDON Black Sea
TURKEY
Mediterranean Sea
Alexandria •
PERSIA
EGYPT ARABIA
Indus River

ALEXANDER THE GREAT
Greece had a second heyday during the rule of the Macedonian Emperor Alexander the Great (356 BC–323 BC). His empire stretched as far as the Indus River, but it collapsed after his death.

THE RISE OF BUDDHISM

MAURYAN
EMPIRE

Arabian
Sea

Bay of
Bengal

IN THE SIXTH CENTURY BC, the
new, peaceful Buddhist faith
appeared in India. To begin with,
the principles of Buddhism
spread slowly, but in the third
century BC, the Indian Emperor
Asoka (d.c.232 BC) became a
Buddhist, and promoted the faith
throughout
his empire.

THE MAURYAN EMPIRE
Chandragupta Maurya led a
revolt against Alexander the
Great's governors in c.322 BC
and established a northern
Indian nation. Chandragupta's
grandson Asoka expanded the
empire southward.

Elaborate
headdress

Rich jewelry

CLASS SYSTEM

From the earliest times,
Indian society has been
divided into four
separate classes.

• Brahmana, the
privileged priest class.

• Kshatriya, the ruling
warrior class.

• Vaisya, the merchant
and land-owning class.

• Sudra, the servant or
peasant class.

MAURYAN CARVING
The Mauryan
period was a golden
age of sculpture,
during which local
styles often
blended with a
Persian influence
that had been
introduced at the
time of Alexander.

YAKSHI OR
FERTILITY GODDESS,
C.300 BC

THE BUDDHA

Buddhism began when a young Indian nobleman, Siddhartha Gautama (563 BC–483 BC), left his life of luxury to find a way to deal with human suffering. In around 528 BC, he found a state of enlightenment (understanding) that he was seeking, and became known as Buddha (the enlightened one).

Buddha

Buddha's mother

WOODEN PLAQUE SHOWING THE BIRTH OF BUDDHA, C.AD 100

ASOKA

Asoka encouraged the spread of Buddhism in India by sending out missionaries and building shrines. He made laws to reduce poverty, which were carved on pillars topped by lions.

THE BEGINNING OF BUDDHISM

Buddha dedicated the rest of his life to teaching his ideas to others. After his death, the faith gradually spread beyond India until it became widespread in many Far Eastern countries.

BUDDHIST CARVING, C.500 BC

SPREAD OF BUDDHISM

DATE	PLACE	INFORMATION
c.AD 50	China	Buddhism reached China during the Han dynasty. It was banned under the T'ang dynasty in 845.
c.550	Japan	Monks from Japan persuaded the Japanese emperor to adopt the faith, making it the country's official religion.
c.600	Tibet	Monks from India converted Tibetan nobles and kings, and the faith was gradually accepted over the next 200 years.

ANCIENT CHINA

CHINA WAS A series of independent states until the country was united under the Ch'in dynasty in 221 BC. This dynasty was short-lived and ended in a period of civil war, after which the strong Han dynasty took over, lasting for four centuries.

PAPER MOLD

PAPER AND PRINTING
The Chinese came up with many inventions long before they were thought of in the West. They guarded the secret of papermaking for 700 years, and also invented a system of printing using woodblocks.

Stone watchtower

THE GREAT WALL
The first Chinese Emperor, Ch'in Shih Huang-ti, joined together existing fortifications to create the 1,400-mile (2,253-km) Great Wall. It provided defense against raiding barbarians from the north. At first, the Great Wall was simply an earth rampart with a wooden fence.

Wooden scaffolding

Core of earth and rubble

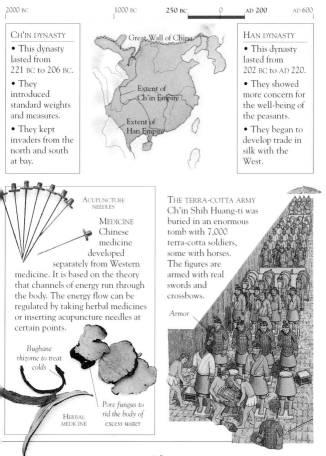

CH'IN DYNASTY

• This dynasty lasted from 221 BC to 206 BC.

• They introduced standard weights and measures.

• They kept invaders from the north and south at bay.

Great Wall of China

Extent of Ch'in Empire

Extent of Han Empire

HAN DYNASTY

• This dynasty lasted from 202 BC to AD 220.

• They showed more concern for the well-being of the peasants.

• They began to develop trade in silk with the West.

ACUPUNCTURE NEEDLES

MEDICINE

Chinese medicine developed separately from Western medicine. It is based on the theory that channels of energy run through the body. The energy flow can be regulated by taking herbal medicines or inserting acupuncture needles at certain points.

Bugbane rhizome to treat colds

HERBAL MEDICINE

Pore fungus to rid the body of excess water

THE TERRA-COTTA ARMY

Ch'in Shih Huang-ti was buried in an enormous tomb with 7,000 terra-cotta soldiers, some with horses. The figures are armed with real swords and crossbows.

Armor

THE ROMANS

FROM ITS BEGINNINGS as a shepherd's village in central Italy, Rome grew into the center of a vast empire. After a period of civil wars, starting in in 49 BC, Octavian (63 BC–AD 14) defeated his rival Mark Antony (82 BC–30 BC) and became the first Roman emperor.

AUGUSTUS
When Julius Caesar's adopted son Octavian became Emperor in 27 BC, he changed his name to Augustus, which means revered.

REPUBLIC IN 200 BC

REPUBLIC IN 133 BC

EMPIRE IN AD 1

THE EXPANSION OF ROME
From its center in Italy, the Roman Empire grew to include most of western Europe and parts of western Asia and northern Africa.

Foresail

Mainsail

TRADING VESSELS
Ships like this Roman corbita brought grain from Egypt and took wine to Gaul (France) and Britain. Spices from the East and slaves from Africa were also regular cargoes.

Cargo hold

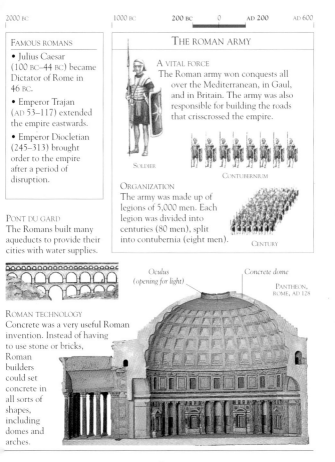

FAMOUS ROMANS

• Julius Caesar (100 BC–44 BC) became Dictator of Rome in 46 BC.

• Emperor Trajan (AD 53–117) extended the empire eastwards.

• Emperor Diocletian (245–313) brought order to the empire after a period of disruption.

PONT DU GARD
The Romans built many aqueducts to provide their cities with water supplies.

ROMAN TECHNOLOGY
Concrete was a very useful Roman invention. Instead of having to use stone or bricks, Roman builders could set concrete in all sorts of shapes, including domes and arches.

THE ROMAN ARMY

A VITAL FORCE
The Roman army won conquests all over the Mediterranean, in Gaul, and in Britain. The army was also responsible for building the roads that crisscrossed the empire.

SOLDIER

CONTUBERNIUM

ORGANIZATION
The army was made up of legions of 5,000 men. Each legion was divided into centuries (80 men), split into contubernia (eight men).

CENTURY

Oculus (opening for light)

Concrete dome

PANTHEON, ROME, AD 128

THE RISE OF CHRISTIANITY

CHRISTIANITY BEGAN as a minority sect in the eastern Mediterranean. Missionaries eventually spread the faith to Rome, but Christians were persecuted there until the fourth century, when the faith was accepted by the Emperor Constantine.

THE FALL OF ROME

The Roman Empire began to decline in the third century.

• The empire was too big to be controlled from one center.

• The emperors relied on army support in order to rule.

• Local barbarian rulers became increasingly powerful.

THE SPREAD OF CHRISTIANITY

In the early fourth century, the king of Axum, a trading empire in northeast Africa, converted to Christianity. By the fifth century, the faith was widespread in Axum.

AXUM OBELISK
c.350

EARLY CHRISTIAN FISH SYMBOL

FRAGMENT OF GOSPEL TEXT

THE BIRTH OF CHRISTIANITY

Christianity is based on the life and teachings of Jesus Christ (c.4 BC–AD 30), which are recorded in the four gospels in the New Testament. Roman and Jewish authorities crucified him because they thought that he was a revolutionary.

EMPEROR CONSTANTINE

PEOPLE WHO HELPED TO SPREAD CHRISTIANITY

NAME	LIFE DATES	INFORMATION
St. Paul	c.AD 3–68	Christian missionary who spread the faith through Arabia, Syria, Greece, and Rome.
Emperor Constantine	280–337	Gave Christians in Rome the freedom to worship.
Emperor Theodosius I	347–395	Made Christianity the official religion of the Roman Empire.

The Byzantine Empire

After the fall of Rome, the eastern capital of the Roman Empire, Byzantium, was renamed Constantinople and became the center of a new Christian empire that lasted until 1453. The core of the Byzantine Empire was modern Turkey and Greece.

Rome •

• Constantinople

BYZANTINE EMPIRE

Mediterranean Sea

BYZANTINE EMPIRE, 565

BYZANTINE ARCHITECTURE
The Byzantines adopted Roman engineering skills, such as building domed roofs. The greatest Byzantine church was the church of Hagia Sophia.

Shallow central dome

Entrance

HAGIA SOPHIA,
CONSTANTINOPLE

BYZANTINE ART
The craft workers of Byzantium were famous for their metalwork, jewelry, and carvings in wood and ivory. This hunting horn is delicately carved from a single elephant tusk.

Carved animals and birds

BYZANTINE
HUNTING HORN

THE LATER EMPIRE

• Justinian I (483–565) reformed laws and brought North Africa and Spain under Byzantine rule.

• In 1204, Crusaders sacked Constantinople.

• Ottoman Turks took Constantinople in 1453, ending the empire.

AMERICAN CIVILIZATIONS

THE AMERICAS WERE HOME to a host of different civilizations. Although they all had distinctive and sophisticated cultures with complex religious and social systems, none of these peoples developed metal-working skills. They used copper, gold, and silver, but mainly for making decorative items. Their tools were made from stone or obsidian (volcanic glass).

MAYA
POTTERY
EFFIGY

THE MAYA
The Central American Maya people built enormous cities with temples on top of enormous stone pyramids. They also built large courts on which they played a form of basketball with a small rubber ball.

PLAYERS OF THE
MAYA BALL GAME

Bridge
handle

POTTERY
JAGUAR,
TIAHUANACO,
C.600

TIAHUANACO
The center of the empire of Tiahuanaco was near Lake Titicaca in Bolivia. Together with the Huari people, its rulers controlled the whole Andean region of South America. Tiahuanaco was a religious center, with many large stone ceremonial buildings.

WHEN AND WHERE

NAME	DATE (HEIGHT)	LOCATION	INFORMATION
Maya	300–900	Peninsula in Mexico and Guatemala	Highly developed culture based in city-states; used stone tools; built pyramids and conducted elaborate religious rituals.
Tiahuanaco	500–1000	Lake Titicaca in Bolivia	Built cities with stone temple enclosures; made masklike sandstone sculpture, and pottery images of gods.
Teotihuacan	100 BC–AD 750	Mexico	City-state on the central Mexican plateau laid out in a grid plan around a temple.
Hopewell	100 BC–AD 600	Mississippi and Ohio River Valleys	Mound-building culture of southern North America.

TEOTIHUACAN

This was one of the most successful cities of central Mexico. The huge site, home to 100,000 people, contained 600 pyramids, 2,000 apartment blocks, and numerous workshops and squares. The people traded with their neighbors, the Maya.

Jaguar symbolizes fertility of soil

JAGUAR GOD, TEOTIHUACAN

HOPEWELL

The North American Hopewell culture has become famous for its large burial mounds. Important Hopewell people were buried in these mounds with lavish grave goods brought from many places in North America.

COPPER BIRD FROM HOPEWELL MOUND

MICA HAND FROM HOPEWELL MOUND

600 TO 1400

TIME CHART

	600	675	750
EVENTS	**600** Height of Maya civilization, Central America ➡ 50 **610** Islamic religion founded ➡ 58 **618** China reunited by T'ang dynasty **622** Year One of Islamic calendar **637** Muslims conquer Jerusalem **642** Islam becomes major religion in Persia **647** Central Asian Hun tribes invade India, causing decline of Gupta Empire	**700** Franks develop feudal system ➡ 60 **c.700** Bantu Africans cross Limpopo River, taking iron-working technology south **c.700** Kingdom of Ghana prospers, West Africa **711** Moors (Muslims) invade Spain ➡ 58 **732** Moors defeated at Tours by Frankish leader Charles Martel (c.688–741), halting Islam's advance in Europe	**751** Muslims defeat Mongols at Samarkand **786** Harun-al-Rashid (766–809) becomes Caliph of Baghdad ➡ 59 **794** Kyoto, ancient capital of Japan, is established **800** Charlemagne (742–814) is crowned first Holy Roman Emperor ➡ 60 **c.800** Polynesian people (Maoris) reach New Zealand BANTU IRONWORKERS, c.700
ARTS & ARCHITECTURE	**618** Golden age of art and literature begins in China **650** Byzantine art and jewelry reaches its peak ➡ 49 BYZANTINE CROSS, 650	**689** Building starts on Dome of the Rock, Jerusalem **700s** Anglo–Saxon epic *Beowulf* written **745** First newspaper printed, China	**785** Building starts on Great Mosque at Córdoba, Spain **792** Building starts on Charlemagne's palace, Aix-la-Chapelle (Aachen), France **c.800** *Book of Kells* produced, Ireland
SCIENCE & INVENTION	**618** Paper money used, China **635** Quill pen first used for writing, Spain **650** Windmill first used, Persia ➡ 59	**700** Porcelain drinking vessels used, China **740** Printing with carved wood blocks developed in Japan and China; it is first used for printing prayers	**751** Arabs learn craft of papermaking from Chinese prisoners ➡ 59 **800s** Viking ships are the fastest ships of their time ➡ 62 **820** Algebra invented, Persian Empire

825	900	975

825

VIKING SHIPS, 800s

844 Kenneth McAlpine (d.858) defeats the Picts and unites Scotland

c.861 Vikings discover Iceland ➡ 63

888 Chola dynasty of Tamil kings replaces Pallavas in southern India and Sri Lanka

848 Great Mosque of Samarra built, Iraq

868 The *Diamond Sutra*, a book of Buddhist scripture is published – the world's oldest printed book

850 Coffee discovered, East Africa

860 Cyrillic alphabet first used, eastern Europe

CHINESE TYPESETTING, 995

900

900 Hausa Kingdom of Daura founded, northern Nigeria

911 Viking leader Rollo (c.860–932) is granted Normandy ➡ 63

920 Ghana's golden age begins

930 Córdoba becomes seat of Arab learning in Spain

950 Polynesian navigator Kupe arrives in New Zealand

960 Sung dynasty takes over China

962 Otto I (912–73) is crowned Holy Roman Emperor ➡ 61

900s Cathedrals built in Romanesque style all over western Europe

900 Organs first installed in abbeys and cathedrals, Europe

910 Benedictine abbey built, Cluny, France

900s Islamic medicine flourishes, Persia ➡ 59

975

980 Arab traders settle on East African coast

980 Toltecs set up capital at Tula, Mexico ➡ 67

c.982 Erik the Red (c.950–c.1010) establishes Viking settlement in Greenland ➡ 63

989 Russians adopt Orthodox Christianity

997 Stephen I (977–1038) becomes King of Hungary

1000 Chimu civilization founded, Peru ➡ 67

c.1000 Viking Leif Erikson reaches the coast of North America ➡ 63

1000–1100 Temple of the Warriors built, Chichén Itzá, Mexico

1001 *Tale of Genji*, the first novel, is written by Japanese noblewoman, Murasaki Shikibu (978–c.1031)

1025 Music first written down as musical notation

995 The Chinese experiment with reusable, movable type

1000 Spinning wheel appears, Asia

1044 Gunpowder invented, China; it is originally used for fireworks

TIME CHART

	1050	1125	1200
EVENTS	**1050** Almoravids (Berber Muslims) begin conquests of Morocco and parts of Spain **1066** William of Normandy (1027–87) defeats English King Harold (c.1020–66) at Battle of Hastings, and takes English throne ➡ 63 **1096** First Crusade begins ➡ 64 **1100** First Iron-Age settlement, Zimbabwe **1104** Crusaders capture Acre, Israel **1119** Bologna University founded, Italy	**1151** Fall of Toltec Empire, Mexico **1155** Paris University founded, France **1156** Civil war by rival clans in Japan leads to domination by samurai warlords **1167** Oxford University founded, England **1169** Saladin (1137–93) becomes ruler of Egypt **1187** Saladin captures Jerusalem from Crusaders **1191** Zen Buddhism introduced to Japan	**c.1200** Cuzco, Peru, becomes an Inca center **1204** Fourth Crusaders sack Constantinople ➡ 64 **1206** Genghis Khan (1162–1227) founds Mongol Empire ➡ 65 **1215** John (1167–1216), King of England seals Magna Carta **1235** Sun Diata (d.1255) founds Mali Empire, West Africa SAMURAI WARRIOR, 1156
ARTS & ARCHITECTURE	**1065** First known stained-glass windows, Augsberg, Germany **1066** Bayeux Tapestry made, France **1115** Philosopher Peter Abelard (1079–1142) begins teaching in Paris	**1132–44** St. Denis Abbey built, France; first complete Gothic church **1174–75** Work begins on Old London Bridge, Avignon Bridge, and Pisa's Leaning Tower	**1200s** Christian churches built, Ethiopia **1200s** Gothic cathedrals built, western Europe **1200s** Great Buddha of Kamakura constructed, Japan **1200s** Many castles built, northern Europe
SCIENCE & INVENTION	**1050** Chinese use gunpowder for warfare **1090** Magnetic compass used, China and Arabia	**1180** Rudder used, Arabia **1190** Saracens use ships with stern rudders CHINESE USE GUNPOWDER, 1050	**1200** Magnifying glass invented, Europe **1200** Windmills used in Europe; the idea may have been brought from Asia by Crusaders **1232** Explosive rockets first used in war between Chinese and Mongols

1250

1250 Mamelukes (rebel slave soldiers) become rulers of Egypt

1250 Maya restore empire and build new capital at Mayapan, Mexico

1271 Marco Polo (1254–1324) sets off from Venice for China

1273 Rudolf Hapsburg (1218–91) becomes ruler of Germany, founding the powerful Hapsburg dynasty ➡ 61

1281 Mongol invaders driven from Japan

1291 Saracens capture Acre, ending Crusades

1300

1300 Incas begin major expansion through Andes ➡ 66

MANSA MUSA

1324 Mansa Musa (d.1332), Emperor of Mali, makes pilgrimage to Mecca

1325 Aztecs found Tenochtitlán, Mexico ➡ 66

1337 Hundred Years War between England and France begins ➡ 68, 69

1347 Black Death reaches Europe ➡ 69

1350

1352 Moroccan scholar Ibn Battuta (1304–68) travels across Sahara to Mali

1358 Jacquerie Revolt: French peasants revolt against raised taxes

1368 Tai Tsu (1328–98) founder of Ming dynasty, drives Mongols from China

1381 Peasants' Revolt, England

1398 Mongol leader Tamerlane (1336–1405) sacks Delhi, India

1250 Lute first brought to Europe from Islamic world

EASTER ISLAND STATUES, 1300s

1300s Statues erected on Easter Island

1300 Giotto (1266–1337) pioneers naturalism in painting

1350 Maoris create rock art, New Zealand

1353 Giovanni Boccaccio (1313–75) writes *The Decameron*

1385 Geoffrey Chaucer (1345–1400) begins to write *The Canterbury Tales*

1250 Longbow invented, Wales ➡ 68

1250 Tinplate first used for armor, Bohemia

1280 Mechanical clock invented, Europe

1290 Eyeglasses invented, Italy

1300 Gunpowder first used in cannons, Europe

1300 Windmills first used to drain land, Netherlands

1320 Lace invented, France and Flanders

1326 Handgun firing bullets first used, Italy

1350 Hand cannon invented, Europe

1350 Mechanical alarm clock invented, Germany

1373 Lock gates first used on Dutch canals to control navigation and drainage

THE RISE OF ISLAM

THE ISLAMIC RELIGION was founded in 610 when the prophet Muhammad (c.570–632) announced that a new faith had been revealed to him. By 750, Muslims (the followers of Islam) conquered a huge Arab Empire, stretching from Persia across North Africa to Spain.

SPAIN

NORTH AFRICA

EGYPT

IRAQ

PERSIA

ARABIA

•Mecca

Arabian Sea

THE SPREAD
OF ISLAM

☐ BY 632

☐ BY 661

☐ BY 750

COPY OF THE KORAN,
1600S

*Leather flap folds
around to protect
book*

*Written in "Naski",
the script most often used
for the Koran*

THE ISLAMIC FAITH
The central beliefs of
Islam are recorded in
the Koran (the
Muslim sacred book).
Muslims believe that
there is only one
God and that
Muhammad is his
prophet. They pray
five times a day while
facing the holy city
of Mecca, and they
fast during the
month of Ramadan.

HARUN-AL-RASHID

Harun-al-Rashid (766–809) was Caliph (ruler) of the Islamic Empire at the height of its power. His court at Baghdad was a center of wealth, business, and culture.

Engraved mortar   *Iron pestle*

PESTLE AND MORTAR FOR MIXING MEDICINES

Enameled earthenware tile

ISLAMIC ARCHITECTURE

The Islamic world developed its own style of architecture. The most typical buildings were mosques with domes and minarets (towers). Inside, a mihrab (niche) showed the direction of Mecca.

ISLAMIC MEDICINE

Islamic doctors treated medicine as a science. They performed minor operations, observed patients carefully, and used many different drugs.

ISLAMIC TECHNOLOGY

DEVELOPMENT		INFORMATION
Windmill, 650s		Windmills worked well on the windswept hills and plains of Persia. Islamic windmills had horizontal sails, but when Muslim colonists took the idea to Spain in the 10th century, they built mills with upright sails.
Lens, 1000s		The Islamic scholar Alhazen (c.965–1039) wrote the earliest reliable description of human vision. He was the first to use the term "lens," although glass lenses were probably not made until 200 years later.
Paper, 751		Paper was invented in China. Some Chinese paper-makers were captured by Muslims invading Samarkand in 751, and the craft of papermaking soon spread around the Islamic Empire.

THE HOLY ROMAN EMPIRE

ON CHRISTMAS DAY 800, the Frankish King Charles I (742–814) was crowned Holy Roman Emperor by the Pope. He was the first ruler to use this title, which was supposed to give him religious authority as well as the power of a great ruler. The core of the empire was modern-day Germany, parts of France, and northern Italy.

FRANKISH THRONE
The Franks took over the Roman province of Gaul (France) in the fifth century.

FEUDAL SYSTEM

The Franks devised the feudal system to run their empire.

• The emperor owned all the land.

• Nobles held land in return for providing services to the emperor.

• Tenants were given use of land in return for services to the nobles.

CHARLEMAGNE
Charles I was known as Charlemagne. He conquered most of western Europe, reformed the legal system, founded schools, and encouraged trade, agriculture, and the arts. His empire broke up about 30 years after his death.

Orb, symbol of monarchy

King rides with no stirrups

BRONZE STATUE OF CHARLEMAGNE ON HORSEBACK, 800s

THE PAPACY
Because the Holy Roman Emperors claimed power over religious matters and the popes wielded great political power, the empire and the papacy were often in conflict over control of Europe.

GREAT MEDIEVAL EMPERORS

NAME	DATES	INFORMATION
Otto I	912–973	Revived the empire and defended it against the invading armies of the Magyars.
Frederick I	1123–1190	Attempted to settle internal conflicts and bring unity to the Holy Roman Empire.
Frederick II	1194–1250	Crusading emperor who secured Jerusalem without fighting, but quarrelled with the Pope.
Rudolf	1218–1291	Duke of Austria who was the first emperor of the Hapsburg dynasty.

IMPERIAL CROWN
After Charlemagne, there was no Holy Roman Emperor until Otto I was crowned in 962. The Holy Roman Empire lasted until 1806, when it was dissolved by Napoleon.

HOLY ROMAN EMPIRE, 987

HOLY ROMAN EMPIRE

THE HAPSBURGS

The Hapsburg family dominated Europe for centuries.

• From 1438 to 1806, every Holy Roman Emperor but one was a Hapsburg.

• Hapsburg power reached its peak with Emperor Charles V (1500–56), who was also King of Spain.

THE VIKINGS

THE VIKINGS SET SAIL from their homelands in Norway, Sweden, and Denmark, raiding the coasts of Europe, plundering the lands, and often settling there. But not all Vikings were raiders. Some traded peacefully, selling goods such as furs, walrus tusks, whale oil, and timber.

BRONZE KEY
A high-ranking Viking would keep his most precious possessions in a strong chest locked with an ornate key.

LONGSHIPS
Viking warships had a single square sail, but could also be rowed. They were the fastest ships of their day.

ANIMAL HEAD
Viking chiefs were sometimes buried in their ships. This animal head was found in a buried Viking ship.

TRADE AND INVASION
Viking merchants sailed around the Mediterranean and along the Dnieper and Volga Rivers. A shortage of farming land at home also led Vikings to set up colonies in Iceland, England, Ireland, and France.

ᚠ ᚢ ᚦ ᚨ ᚱ ᚲ ᚺ ᚾ ᛁ ᚨ ᛋ ᛏ ᛒ ᛗ ᛚ ᚱ

F U TH A R K H N I A S T B M L R

VIKING RUNES
The Viking alphabet was known as the "futhark," after the first six runes (letters).

THOR'S HAMMER LUCKY CHARM, 1100S

Ring to attach chain

VIKING COSTUME
In their cold homelands, Vikings wore warm woolen garments fastened with metal clasps and brooches. Fur trimmings provided extra warmth.

Leather purse

Gold brooch

RELIGION
The many Viking gods included Odin, the god of war; Frigg, the goddess of childbirth; and Thor, the god of thunder. According to legend, Thor's main weapon was his magic hammer.

EXPLORERS
• In c.861, Ingolf was the first Viking to reach Iceland.

• In c.982, Erik the Red (c.950–c.1010) reached Greenland and founded settlements.

• Erik's son Leif reached North America in c.1000. He called the new land Vinland (wineland).

THE NORMANS
In 911, the Viking Rollo (c.860–932) was granted land in northern France by the French king. Rollo and his followers were the first Normans. They took control of Sicily (1072–91) and England (1066). Under England's first Norman king, William I (1027–87), the Normans built strong castles like this one.

ROCHESTER CASTLE, ENGLAND

EUROPE AND THE EAST

DURING THE 12TH AND 13TH centuries,
religious tensions between Europeans
and the Turks of western Asia led to
the Crusades. Meanwhile, Europe's
eastern borders were threatened by
the powerful Mongol Empire.

MILITARY ORDERS
These are the shields of
the Hospitallers and the
Teutonic Knights, orders
of fighting monks.

The Crusades

In 1095, Pope Urban II (c.1042–99) preached a sermon in which
he encouraged Western leaders to recapture the holy lands of
western Asia from the Muslim Turks. The result was a series of
religious wars known as the Crusades.

MAJOR CRUSADES		
CRUSADE	DATE	OUTCOME
First Crusade	1096–1099	Crusaders take Antioch, then Jerusalem in July 1099.
Second Crusade	1147–1149	Poor leadership results in Crusaders' defeat in Anatolia.
Third Crusade	1189–1192	Crusaders take control of eastern Mediterranean coast.
Fourth Crusade	1202–1204	Crusaders plunder Constantinople; they do not reach the Holy Land.

CRUSADER
The cross sewn to the
crusader's surcoat and
shield showed that he
was fighting for God.

SARACEN
Muslim warriors
(Saracens) carried a
round shield and a
curved scimitar.

Surcoat

Chain-mail shirt

Scimitar

The Mongol Empire

At the end of the 12th century,
a number of tribes from central Asia
joined up under the leader Temujin
(1162–1227) to form a Mongol army.
They fought their way eastward,
quickly amassing a huge empire.
Temujin was renamed Genghis Khan,
(Absolute Ruler).

MONGOL LANDS

   EMPIRE OF GENGHIS KHAN, C.1227

   EMPIRE OF KUBLAI KHAN, C.1294

   LANDS OF BOTH GENGHIS
   AND KUBLAI

Bows with armor-piercing arrows

MONGOL
CAVALRYMEN

MONGOL WARRIORS
The key to the Mongols'
military success was their
cavalry. Mongol horsemen could
fire arrows while riding at full
speed. They could also travel fast
– up to 75 miles (120 km) a day.

ARROWS
Mongol soldiers
used arrows with
whistling heads to
signal during battle.

Holes

Embroidered pattern

Flowers

TRADE WITH THE WEST
The Mongols controlled trade with
the West by policing the Silk Road,
a network of trade routes across Asia.
Merchants exported silk, porcelain,
lacquered goods, spices, and tea.

CHINESE SILK

AZTECS AND INCAS

THE AZTECS, WHO BUILT their empire through war, diplomacy, and trade, settled in Mexico in the 13th century. The Incas were a warrior tribe who came to power in the Andes. By the 15th century, these two empires dominated Central and South America.

Great temple

Temple of Quetzalcoatl

Temple of the Sun

Ball court

TENOCHTITLÁN
The Aztec capital, Tenochtitlán, was built on swampy land in Lake Texcoco. Three causeways linked it to the shore of the lake.

Tenochtitlán

AZTEC EMPIRE

Gulf of Mexico

Pacific Ocean

INCA EMPIRE

20 days of the Aztec month

AZTEC AND INCA EMPIRES
The Aztecs ruled a compact empire in central Mexico. The Incas built a network of roads to improve communications in their large empire.

AZTEC SUN STONE
The Aztecs believed that the world had passed through four previous phases, and that the Sun, the Moon, and humanity were created in the fifth phase. This stone shows the Sun, the four previous phases of creation, and the 20 days of the Aztec month.

INCA QUIPU

Unlike most other highly developed civilizations, the Incas had no system of writing. Instead, they worked out a way of recording information using knotted lengths of string called quipus.

Colors record different types of information

Knots record numbers

RISE AND FALL

• The Aztec Empire reached its height in the 1420s. It fell to Spanish invaders (conquistadors) in 1520.

• The Incas grew in power in the early 1400s. Their empire was destroyed by the Spanish in 1532.

CEREMONIAL KNIFE

Knives like this were used to perform human sacrifices, which were an important part of Inca religion.

OTHER AMERICAN PEOPLES

THE TOLTECS

Before the Aztecs came to power, the Toltecs dominated many Mexican cities. Their capital was at Tula. Like the Aztecs and the Maya, the Toltecs grew maize, built pyramid temples, and performed human sacrifices.

Priest

CHIMU BURIAL CEREMONY

King is carried to his burial place in sitting position

TOLTEC SACRIFICE

THE CHIMU

The Chimu ruled northern Peru until the 15th century. They built a network of roads leading to their capital, Chan Chan.

THE HUNDRED YEARS WAR

WHEN EDWARD III (1312–77) was crowned
King of England in 1327, he thought
he also had a good claim to the
French throne through his mother.
In 1337, he declared war on France,
beginning a conflict that was to last
over a hundred years, until the final
French victory in 1453.

LONGBOWS
Longbows fired armor-
piercing arrows and were
quicker to load than
crossbows.

THE SIEGE OF ORLÉANS
A turning point in the war came
with the siege of this city in
1429. The English cut the city
off for seven months, but
French leader Joan of Arc
attacked the English and
broke the siege.

*English
troops guard
approaches
to city*

*French troops
mount an attack*

CHAIN MAIL
In the 14th century,
soldiers wore shirts made
of linked iron rings.

LEADERS OF THE HUNDRED YEARS WAR		
NAME	LIFE DATES	INFORMATION
Edward, the Black Prince	1330–1376	Son of Edward III who fought at the Battle of Crécy (1346) and captured the French king at Poitiers (1356).
Henry V	1387–1422	English king who defeated the French at Agincourt (1415) and was made heir to the French throne.
Joan of Arc	1412–1431	Inspirational French leader who was eventually burned at the stake at Rouen, charged with heresy.

PHASES OF THE WAR

- From 1337 to 1360, the English won much French territory.

- From 1364 to 1380, the French under Charles V (1337–80) began to reconquer lost lands.

- From 1420 to 1452, the French regained all their lost territory, except Calais.

The Black Death

In 1347, an epidemic swept across Europe. In four years, some 25 million people (about a quarter of the population) died of the Black Death, a combination of pneumonic and bubonic plague.

SPREAD OF THE PLAGUE
The Black Death was carried by fleas that lived on rats. The epidemic originated in Asia and rapidly spread to Europe along trade routes. Only a few areas escaped the dreadful disease, including parts of Poland, Flanders, southwest France, and Milan.

1400 TO 1750

TIME CHART

	1400	1435	1470
EVENTS	**1400s** Expansion of Inca and Aztec Empires ➡ 66, 67 **1400s** Trading empires flourish, Africa ➡ 85 **1404** Chinese navigator Cheng Ho (1371–1435) sets off on his first voyage ➡ 79 **1405** Fall of Mongol Empire **1415** Battle of Agincourt: English defeat French ➡ 69 **1429** Joan of Arc (1412–31) leads French at Siege of Orléans ➡ 68, 69	**1450** Machu Picchu founded, Peru **1453** End of Hundred Years War ➡ 68, 69 **1453** Fall of Constantinople ends Byzantine Empire ➡ 49, 82 JOAN OF ARC **1455–85** Wars of the Roses, England; royal houses of Lancaster and York fight over rival claims to the throne **1464** Sonni Ali (d.1492) becomes ruler of Songhai, West Africa	**1479** Spain united under Ferdinand of Aragon (1452–1516) and Isabella of Castile (1451–1504) ➡ 78 **1480** Spanish Inquisition starts ➡ 78 **1485** Henry VII (1457–1509) becomes first Tudor King of England and Wales after Battle of Bosworth ends Wars of the Roses **1492** Italian explorer Christopher Columbus (1451–1506) reaches Americas
ARTS & ARCHITECTURE	**1400s** Oil painting becomes popular as patrons demand pictures such as portraits **1400s** Renaissance begins in Italy ➡ 76, 77	**1446** Dome of Florence Cathedral completed, Italy **c.1450** Building at Great Zimbabwe, Africa, at its height **1456** First printed Bible	MING BOWL, 1490s **1488** Ming emperor orders rebuilding of Great Wall of China **1490s** Chinese blue-and-white Ming porcelain exported to Europe
SCIENCE & INVENTION	GREAT ZIMBABWE, C.1450 **1405** Metal screw used, Germany **1410** Coil spring used in clocks, Italy	**1451** Printing with metal movable type invented; printing presses are rapidly set up all over Europe	**1470** Mariner's astrolabe invented, Europe **1495** Double entry bookkeeping invented, Venice, Italy **1498** Toothbrush first used, China

1500	1535	1570
1517 Reformation begins, Europe ➡ 80, 81	**1542** Portuguese traders reach Japan	**1571** Ottoman fleet defeated at Battle of Lepanto
1519–32 Aztec and Inca empires destroyed ➡ 67, 86	**1553** Lady Jane Grey (1537–54) is Queen of England for nine days	**1572** St. Bartholomew's Day Massacre of Protestants, France ➡ 81
1520 Suleiman (1494–1566) becomes Ottoman emperor ➡ 82	**1556** Akbar (1542–1605) becomes Mogul Emperor of India ➡ 83	**1577–80** Francis Drake (c.1545–96) sails around the world
1522 After death of Ferdinand Magellan (1480–1521), his crew complete first around-the-world voyage	**1556** Philip II (1527–98) becomes King of Spain ➡ 81	**1588** English fleet defeats Spanish Armada ➡ 81
1534 Henry VIII (1491–1547) creates Church of England ➡ 81	**1558** Elizabeth I (1533–1603) becomes Queen of England	
1534 St Ignatius Loyola (1491–1556) founds Jesuit order		SPANISH ARMADA, 1588

1503 Leonardo da Vinci (1452–1519) begins to paint the *Mona Lisa*	**1552** François Rabelais (c.1494–c.1553) completes *Gargantua and Pantagruel*	**1590** El Greco (1541–1614) paints *St. Jerome*
1512 Michelangelo Buonarotti (1475–1564) completes Sistine Chapel frescoes, Italy	**1555–60** St. Basil's Cathedral built, Moscow	**1590** William Shakespeare (1564–1616) begins to write plays
	1559–84 Building of palace of Escorial, Madrid, Spain	**1594** First opera, *Dafne* by Jacopo Peri (1561–1633), produced

1509 Wallpaper first used, England	**1543** Nicolas Copernicus (1473–1543) states that Earth and the other planets orbit the Sun	**1573** Potatoes first brought to Europe from Peru
1511 Watch invented, Germany		**1592** Galileo Galilei (1564–1642) invents the thermometer
1519 Chocolate first brought to Europe from Mexico	**1569** Gerhard Kremer Mercator (1512–94) creates his new world map on a projection still used today	
1530 Corks used to stop bottles, western Europe		POTATO PLANT, 1573

7 3

TIME CHART

	1600	1625	1650
EVENTS	**1600** Tokugawa period begins, Japan ➡84 **1600–14** English, Dutch, Danish, and French East India Companies founded ➡86, 87 **1603** James VI (1566–1625) of Scotland becomes James I of England **1618** Thirty Years War begins, Europe **1620** *Mayflower* sails to America	**1626** Dutch found New Amsterdam (now New York) THE MAYFLOWER, 1620 **1642** Explorer Abel Tasman (1603–59) reaches Tasmania and New Zealand **1642–49** English Civil War ➡88 **1643** Reign of Louis XIV (1638–1715) begins, France ➡88 **1644** Manchu dynasty founded, China ➡89 **1649** Charles I (b.1600) executed, England ➡88	**1653–58** Protectorate of Oliver Cromwell (1599–1658), England **1658** Reign of Aurangzeb (1618–1707), last great Mogul emperor, begins, India **1660** Charles II (1630–85) restored to English throne **1664** English seize New Amsterdam from Dutch and rename it New York **1665** Great Plague in London **1666** Great Fire of London
ARTS & ARCHITECTURE	**1603** Kabuki theater begins, Japan **1605** First part of *Don Quixote* by Miguel Cervantes (1547–1616) published **1606** Building of Blue Mosque starts, Istanbul	**1632** Building of Taj Mahal begins, India **1636** High point of Flemish and Dutch art TAJ MAHAL, 1632	**1656** Piazza of St. Peter's built, Rome **1661** Building of Palace of Versailles begins, France ➡88
SCIENCE & INVENTION	**1619–28** William Harvey (1578–1657) investigates blood circulation **1623** First mechanical calculator invented, Germany **1624** Primitive submarine demonstrated in Thames River, London	**1632** Galileo supports the theory that the Earth and other planets orbit the Sun; in 1633, he is forced by the Inquisition to retract his support **1637** Umbrella made from oiled cloth, France	**1650** Vacuum pump invented, Germany **1656** Pendulum clock invented, Netherlands **1661** First banknotes issued by Bank of Sweden **1667** First successful blood transfusion, France

1675

1675 War between colonists and Native Americans devastates New England

1677 Ottoman Empire at war with Russia

1682 Reign of Peter the Great (1672–1725) begins, Russia ➡89

1689 William of Orange (1650–1702) becomes joint sovereign of Britain with his wife, Mary II (1662–94)

1690s Asante kingdom established on Gold Coast, Africa ➡85

1692 Salem witch trials, New England

1700

1700s Enlightenment begins, Europe ➡96, 97

1701–13 Much of Europe is involved in War of Spanish Succession, which begins after death of Charles II of Spain (1665–1700)

1707 Act of Union joins England and Scotland

1715 Jacobites rise up and attempt to restore Stuart king to British throne

1721 Robert Walpole (1676–1745) becomes first British prime minister

ST. PETERSBURG, 1703

1725

1727 Border fixed between China and Russia

1737 Earthquake kills 300,000 people, India

1739 Spain and Britain fight for control of North American and Caribbean waters

1740 Frederick the Great (1712–86) becomes King of Prussia

1741 Vitus Bering (1681–1741) discovers strait between Russia and Alaska

1746 Battle of Culloden ends second Jacobite rising, Scotland

---

1675 Rebuilding of St. Paul's Cathedral, London begins, to a design by Christopher Wren (1632–1723)

1677 Jean Racine (1639–99) writes his tragedy *Phèdre*

1703 St. Petersburg founded, Russia

1709 Piano invented, Italy

1717 Georg Friederich Handel (1685–1759) writes his *Water Music*

1726 *Gulliver's Travels* by Jonathan Swift (1667–1745) published

1729 Johann Sebastian Bach (1685–1750) writes his choral work *St. Matthew Passion*

1675 Pocket watch invented, Netherlands

1675 Scientist and astronomer, Isaac Newton (1642–1727) experiments with static electricity ➡96

1712 Steam engine invented, England

1714 Mercury thermometer invented, Germany

ISAAC NEWTON

1733 Mechanized weaving invented, England

1733 Natural rubber discovered in rain forests of Peru

1741 Centigrade scale first used on thermometers

THE RENAISSANCE

IN THE 14TH AND 15TH CENTURIES, the Renaissance, a rebirth of interest in the culture of ancient Greece and Rome, began in northern Italy and spread throughout Europe. Scholars and artists were inspired by the rediscovery of Greek and Roman ideas about art, literature, and science.

LORENZO DE MEDICI MEDALLION

PATRONS
Rich, noble families such as the Medicis ruled Italian city-states. Many of them showed off their wealth and status by becoming sponsors of the artists.

CLASSICAL STYLE
Architects turned their back on the gothic style of the Middle Ages. New buildings followed the proportions of the buildings of ancient Greece and Rome. The exteriors were decorated with columns, and they were often roofed with domes.

Dome designed by Michelangelo

Cupola (small dome)

Triangular pediment

Corinthian column

BASILICA OF ST. PETER'S, ROME, 1506–1626

RENAISSANCE FAMILIES
• The Medicis ruled Florence from 1434 to 1737. Their wealth came from banking.

• The Borgias were powerful in Rome in the 15th and 16th centuries. Two of the Borgias became popes.

THE SCHOOL OF ATHENS, BY RAPHAEL, 1511

Aristotle

Philosophers of ancient Greece

Plato

Statue is 18 ft (5.49 m) high

Dressed in the clothes of ancient Greece

DAVID, BY MICHELANGELO, 1504

VISUAL ARTS

As well as religious themes and portraits of their patrons, artists portrayed subjects from ancient history and mythology. All were painted and sculpted with realism. A new interest in the human form was evident.

SCIENCE AND TECHNOLOGY

• Printing with metal movable type was invented by German goldsmith Johannes Gutenberg (1400–68) in 1451.

• Italian artist and inventor Leonardo da Vinci (1452–1519) made designs for a helicopter, a parachute, and a flying machine with flapping wings.

PEOPLE OF THE RENAISSANCE

NAME	DATES	INFORMATION
Desiderius Erasmus	1469–1536	Dutch scholar, philosopher, and writer; translator of New Testament.
Niccolò Machiavelli	1469–1527	Italian statesman and writer of books on government.
Michelangelo Buonarotti	1475–1564	Italian painter, sculptor, architect, and poet.
Andreas Vesalius	1514–1564	Belgian writer of first accurate book on human anatomy.

SPAIN AND PORTUGAL

IN THE 15TH CENTURY, Spain and Portugal were two of the most powerful countries in Europe. They both began to set up great world empires.

ARCH, THE ALHAMBRA, 1334–54

Reconquest of Spain

From the 11th century onward, Christian leaders of various Spanish regions began to recapture parts of the country from its Islamic rulers. By 1248, most of Spain had been recovered.

ISLAMIC SPAIN
The Muslims had constructed many fine buildings in Spain, including the palace of the Alhambra in Granada.

Inscription

RELIGIOUS INTOLERANCE

• Ferdinand and Isabella set up the Spanish Inquisition to seek out heretics.

• Thousands of Jews were given the choice of becoming Christian or leaving Spain.

UNITED SPAIN
In 1479, Spain was united after the marriage of Ferdinand of Aragon (1452–1516) and Isabella of Castille (1451–1504).

Exploration

In 1416, Portuguese Prince
Henry the Navigator
(1394–1460) founded
a school of navigation
and began to send
out ships to explore
the coast of Africa.

Triangular sails

PORTUGUESE CARAVEL,
1400S

PORTUGAL

AFRICA

INDIA

Atlantic
Ocean

DIAZ
1487–88

DA GAMA
1498

Indian
Ocean

SOUTH
AMERICA

CABRAL
1500

Cape of
Good Hope

ROUTES OF THE EXPLORERS
Portuguese navigators
traveled the world in search
of new sea routes. They
traveled in caravels, ships that
were only about 66 ft (20 m)
long, but had large holds to
carry all that they needed on
a long voyage.

Pepper

Sweet potato

Kidney bean

Pineapple

Potato

Peanut

Tomato

FRUITS OF
EXPLORATION
In the Americas,
explorers came
across many
types of fruits
and vegetables
that were new
to them.

CHINESE EXPLORER

Between 1404 and
1433, Chinese
navigator Cheng Ho
(1371–1435) led seven
expeditions westwards
from China to explore
India and East Africa
and extend Chinese
influence abroad.

THE REFORMATION

CORRUPTION WITHIN the Catholic Church during the 16th century sparked off a religious movement called the Reformation. Violent conflicts broke out between Catholics and the reformers, who were known as Protestants. All over Europe, new churches were set up.

Luther's 95 theses

MARTIN LUTHER
German reformer Martin Luther (1483–1546) objected to the Catholic Church's sale of indulgences, which were promises of God's forgiveness in return for money. In 1517, Luther compiled a list of 95 theses (arguments) against indulgences and nailed it to the church door at Wittenberg.

Martin Luther

Heretic being burned at stake

RELIGIOUS UPHEAVAL
People who wanted to worship in a different way or who attacked the power of the Catholic Church were often severely punished. Some were even burned alive.

REFORMATION AIMS
• Religious teachings should be based more closely on the words of the Bible.
• The Bible should be translated into major European languages.

PHILIP II OF SPAIN

THE SPANISH ARMADA

In 1588, Philip (1527–98) sent a fleet, the Spanish Armada, to invade England so that he could restore Catholic rule. The Armada was defeated, and England remained Protestant.

DAGGER OF HENRY IV OF FRANCE

THE FRENCH STRUGGLE

After years of religious conflict, Protestant King Henry IV (1553–1610) established religious toleration in France.

GERMAN PEASANTS' WAR

Encouraged by the teachings of Luther, German peasants rose up against their lords in 1524, demanding better conditions. They hoped for Luther's support, but he supported the lords. Within a year, the revolt was crushed.

Soldiers crush the revolt mercilessly

REFORMATION EVENTS

EVENT	DATE	INFORMATION
English break with Rome	1534	Henry VIII (1491–1547) wanted to divorce his first wife, but divorce was not permitted under Catholicism, so Henry took over the English Church himself.
Dutch rebellions	1568–1648	The Netherlands were part of the Catholic Empire, but the mainly Protestant Dutch wanted to be independent. After numerous rebellions, independence came in 1648.
St Bartholomew's Day Massacre, France	1572	In a clash between Huguenots (Protestants) and Catholics, thousands of Protestant men, women, and children were killed, both in Paris and the provinces.

NEW EMPIRES

SEVERAL LARGE EMPIRES in Asia and Africa reached
their height in the 16th century. The Ottoman
and Mogul Empires were ruled by strong
Muslim leaders who established efficient
new systems of government.

*Stylized patterns
show Chinese
influence*

Ottoman Empire

Ottoman (Turkish) rulers considered it their
duty to conquer other peoples and convert
them to Islam. By the reign of Suleiman I
(1494–1566), the empire was one of
the most powerful ever known, and
stretched across three continents:
Asia, Europe, and Africa.

OTTOMAN
EMPIRE
Istanbul
TURKEY

AFRICA

ART
The artistic styles
of peoples within
the expanding
empire influenced
Ottoman artists
and craft workers.

SULEIMAN I
A renowned
military leader,
Suleiman was
known to his
people as
al-Qanuni
or the Law-giver.

EXTENT OF THE EMPIRE
The Ottomans conquered the
Byzantine city of Constantinople in
1453. They renamed it Istanbul, and
made it the capital of their vast empire.

DAGGER
Worn just for show rather than as a weapon, this dagger is beautifully engraved with lines of poetry.

Engraved calligraphy   *Steel blade*

OTTOMAN GOVERNMENT
• Suleiman presided over a civil service staffed with highly trained officials.
• The top officials were slaves who had been trained for their government jobs from childhood.

Mogul Empire

In 1500, India was divided up into warring Hindu and Muslim states. Descendants of the Mongols, the Muslim Moguls swept down from the north and took over much of India, which they ruled until 1858.

MOGUL EMPIRE
1605
Arabian Sea   1700   *Bay of Bengal*

AKBAR
Although Emperor Akbar (1542–1605) was a Muslim, he was tolerant of other religions, and allowed people to worship freely.

Akbar discussing religious beliefs

EXTENT OF THE EMPIRE
At its greatest extent in 1700, the Mogul Empire reached almost to the southern tip of India.

Tokugawa Japan

Japan's head of state was the emperor, but the most powerful person was actually the shogun, who ruled on his behalf. In the late 16th century, politician and general Tokugawa Ieyasu (1543–1616) defeated his rivals and became shogun. The Tokugawa family continued to rule Japan until 1867.

WEAPONRY
A samurai carried two swords and a dagger.

Armor

Bow

JAPANESE CASTLE
The shogun ruled with the help of local lords called daimyo. The daimyo built castles from which they could control their local area.

Wooden upper story

Narrow window openings

Plastered wall

Wooden shingles

Gun loop

SAMURAI
The Samurai were trained warriors who served a lord and kept law and order.

FOREIGN RELATIONS
By 1650, Japan's only contact with the outside world was through Dutch and Chinese trading posts like this one.

African empires

African states such as the Mali and
Songhai Empires grew wealthy from trade
in goods such as gold, copper, and salt.
These empires were often held together by
a combination of a strong ruler and an
effective legal system.

RELIGION AND CULTURE
- Many North African empires were mainly Muslim.
- Universities were set up at the trading centers of Jenne and Timbuktu in the Songhai Empire.
- African empires built large walled cities with mosques.

SONGHAI MOSQUE
This mud-brick mosque
was first built in the
14th century.

Eagles
adorned the
throne of
an Ashanti
king

ASHANTI GOLD
The Ashanti people created and
traded beautiful gold objects. They
used magnificent gold sculptures to
show the power of their kings.

The shape of
feathers is
visible in the
elaborately
worked gold

GREAT EMPIRES OF AFRICA

EMPIRE	HEIGHT	INFORMATION
Mali	1200–1400	Large, Muslim West African empire, with an efficient legal system and many trading links.
Benin	1200–1900	Kingdom in West Africa, famous for its superb craftsmanship in the wood, stone, and bronze.
Songhai	1400–1600	Great Muslim trading empire that grew from its base in Mali to include large areas of West Africa.
Ashanti	1600–1900	West African state that set up an African coastal trading network.

ASHANTI
SCULPTURE

COLONY AND TRADE

JOURNEY OF explorers in the 15th and 16th centuries gave European traders new routes to the Far East and new trade destinations. Organizations such as the East India Companies of France, England, and the Netherlands set up trading stations in the Far East, which eventually became colonies. European settlers went on to found colonies all over the world.

Pacific Ocean

Atlantic Ocean

CANADA

NEW SPAIN

LOUISIANA

THIRTEEN COLONIES

NEW GRANADA

BRAZIL

PERU

RIO DE LA PLATA

NORTH AMERICA
Europeans began to colonize North America from the late 15th century. Many settlers were escaping from religious persecution. They led a simple farming life.

SOUTH AND CENTRAL AMERICA
After the overthrow of the Aztec and Inca Empires, Spanish and Portuguese settlers began to colonize South and Central America.

Spaniard

Inca

COLONIES AND TRADE
ROUTES, 1700

ENGLAND

FRANCE

NETHERLANDS

PORTUGAL

SPAIN

→ TRADE ROUTE

ENGLAND
NETHERLANDS
FRANCE
SPAIN
PORTUGAL

AFRICA

INDIA

Indian
Ocean

PORTUGUESE

ENGLISH   DUTCH

FRENCH

SPANISH

INDONESIA

NEW HOLLAND

AFRICA
European slave traders shipped
African people to the Americas,
the Caribbean, Asia, and Europe to
become slaves on plantations and
in mines. By 1800, half of Brazil's
population was of African origin.

PLAN OF SLAVE SHIP — Slaves crammed in
with no space to move

INDIA AND
THE FAR EAST
The Portuguese
dominated the spice
trade in the Far East
for a century, but
in the early 17th
century, the
English, French,
and Dutch East
India Companies
began to compete.

PEPPER

CLOVES

Mace

NUTMEG

DUTCH EAST
INDIA OFFICER

ABSOLUTE RULERS

DURING THE 17TH AND 18TH CENTURIES, Europe was dominated by monarchs who ruled with absolute power. This meant that they had total control over every aspect of their country, and could make reforms, raise taxes, or start wars without consulting anyone else.

LOUIS XIV

LOUIS XIV
In France, Louis XIV (1638–1715) proved to be an effective absolute ruler. He used regional officials to rule the country, reduced the power of the nobles, and made France the most powerful country in Europe. However, because Louis led an extravagant life and waged expensive wars, he had to raise taxes, which were a burden to the ordinary people of France.

CHARLES I
The monarch of England traditionally ruled with the help of Parliament, but Charles I (1600–49) believed that he had the right to disregard Parliament. He ruled with absolute power for 11 years. Then in 1642, Charles' poor relationship with Parliament sparked a civil war. Charles and his supporters were defeated, and the king was executed in 1649. England became a republic until 1660.

CHARLES I

VERSAILLES
Louis brought many nobles to live in his palace at Versailles, where they could be easily controlled.

EXECUTION OF CHARLES I

THE DIVINE RIGHT OF KINGS
For hundreds of years, European monarchs claimed that they had been given the right to rule their countries by God. They believed that this meant they could rule as absolute monarchs, and that no one had the right to question their actions. All opposition to these monarchs was firmly suppressed.

RETAINING POWER
• Powerful nobles were observed closely and kept busy with state ceremonies.

• Potential rebels were sent away on long diplomatic missions.

PETER THE GREAT
The greatest of all the Russian czars, Peter the Great (1672–1725), founded the city of St. Petersburg. He brought western ideas, culture, and technology to Russia and reformed education, the civil service, the church, and the army. He warned Russian boyars (nobles) that they should not take their power for granted, and ordered that their traditional beards should be cut off to show that change was in the air.

CHINESE
FIGURE

THE MANCHUS
In 1644, the Manchu dynasty was founded in China. Early Manchu emperors crushed the resistance of the supporters of the preceding Ming dynasty and encouraged the arts and learning. The climax of the dynasty came with the reign of Quianlong (1736–96). He increased Chinese power in central Asia by defeating the Mongols and opening up trade routes to Europe.

Embroidered silk robe

Russian boyar

K'ANG HSI, THE SECOND
MANCHU EMPEROR

1750 TO 1900

	1750	1765	1780
EVENTS	**1750** China conquers Tibet **1755** Earthquake at Lisbon, Portugal **1756–63** Seven Years War in Europe: Britain and Germany victorious **1757** Battle of Plassey: British conquer Bengal **1759** Battle of Quebec: British win control of Canada from French **1762** Catherine the Great (1729–96) begins reign in Russia **1763** Pontiac (1720–69) leads Native American uprising in North America	**1768** Ali Bey (d.1773) becomes ruler of independent Egypt **1769** Richard Arkwright (1732–92) builds first cotton factory **1770** James Cook (1728–79) reaches Australia ➡97 **1771** Russia conquers Crimea **1773** Boston Tea Party: North American colonists protest against taxes **1775–83** American Revolution ➡98, 99 **1776** Declaration of Independence, US	**1787–89** United States Constitution and Bill of Rights written and ratified ➡99 **1788** British colony of New South Wales founded, Australia **1789** Storming of the Bastille begins French Revolution ➡100 **1791** Revolution in Haiti by Pierre Toussaint L'Ouverture (1743–1803) ➡99 **1792–1815** Napoleonic Wars in Europe led by Napoleon Bonaparte (1769–1821) ➡101
ARTS & ARCHITECTURE	**1751–86** *L'Encyclopédie*, the world's first encyclopedia, published, France ➡96 **1764** Eight-year-old Wolfgang Amadeus Mozart (1756–91) composes his first symphony	MOZART	**1780** Johann Wolfgang von Goethe (1749–1832) pioneers Romantic movement in art and literature **1792** Mary Wollstonecraft (1759–97) writes *Vindication of the Rights of Women*
SCIENCE & INVENTION	**1752** Lightning conductor invented by Benjamin Franklin (1706–90) ➡97 **1757** Sextant invented by John Campbell (1720–90) ➡97	**1769** Rotary steam engine patented by James Watt (1736–1819) **1777** Antoine Lavoisier (1743–94) shows that air is made mainly of oxygen and nitrogen	**1783** Étienne (1745–99) and Joseph (1740–1810) Montgolfier launch their hot-air balloon ➡97 **1792** Guillotine used for executions, France ➡100 GUILLOTINE, 1792

1795	1810	1825
1795 French Directoire government set up	**1810–22** Many South American countries gain independence ➜103	**1830** British and Boers clash in South Africa
1801 Union of Great Britain and Ireland	**1812–14** Britain and US at war	**1830** French invade Algeria
1804 British win control of Cape of Good Hope	**1814** Congress of Vienna restores European monarchies	**1830** July Revolution overthrows Charles X (1757–1836) of France
1804 Napoleon becomes Emperor of France ➜101	**1815** Battle of Waterloo: Napoleon defeated ➜101	**1832** First Reform Act extends voting rights in Britain
1805 Battle of Austerlitz: Napoleon defeats Russian and Austrian forces	**1821–29** Greek War of Independence from Turkey	**1836** Great Trek of Boer farmers to establish independent Transvaal, South Africa
1805 British admiral Horatio Nelson (1758–1805) destroys French fleet at Battle of Trafalgar ➜101	**1824–27** First Ashanti War between British and Ashanti of Gold Coast	**1836** Texas wins independence from Mexico
		1837 Victoria (1819–1901) becomes Queen of England

NAPOLEON

1790 William Wordsworth (1770–1850) and Samuel Coleridge (1772–1834) found the English Romantic movement	**1810** Greek revival architecture becomes popular in western Europe	**1832** Goethe completes *Faust*
1800 John Constable (1776–1837) pioneers painting outdoors	**1812** Brothers Jakob (1785–1863) and Wilhelm (1786–1859) Grimm publish their collection of fairy tales	**1834** Munich Glypothek, first specially built museum, completed
	PASSENGER RAILROAD, 1825	**1836–7** Charles Dickens (1812–70) publishes his first novel, *The Pickwick Papers*

1796 First vaccination given by Edward Jenner (1749–1823)		**1825** First passenger railroad opens, England ➜105
1800 Battery invented by Alessandro Volta (1745–1827)	**1812** Tin can invented by Nicolas Appert (1750–1841)	**1827** Photography pioneered by Joseph-Nicéphore Niepce (1765–1833)
1803 Steam locomotive invented by Richard Trevithick (1771–1883)	**1816** Stethoscope invented by René Laënnec (1781–1826)	**1839** Louis Daguerre (1789–1851) develops his photographic technique
	1821 Electric motor invented by Michael Faraday (1791–1867) ➜105	

TIME CHART

	1840	1850	1860
EVENTS	**1840** Treaty of Waitingi: British return ancient Maori land rights **1842** Treaty of Nanking opens Chinese ports to British trade and gives Hong Kong to Britain **1846** Potato famine begins, Ireland ➡103 **1846–48** Mexican–American War: US victorious **1847** Bantus defeated by British in southern Africa **1848** California Gold Rush **1848** Year of revolutions in Europe ➡102	DAVID LIVINGSTONE **1851** Australian Gold Rush **1853** US forces Japan to open up to foreign trade **1853–56** Crimean War: Britain and France defeat Russia **1855** David Livingstone (1813–73) reaches Victoria Falls, sparking off European exploration of African interior **1857** Indian Mutiny: Indians rebel against British	**1860–70** Maoris fight settlers in New Zealand **1861–65** American Civil War ➡106, 107 **1864** International Red Cross founded **1866** Austro–Prussian War: Austria defeated **1867** Dominion of Canada created **1867** Mexicans force French to withdraw from Mexico
ARTS & ARCHITECTURE	**1847** *Jane Eyre*, by Charlotte Brontë (1816–55), published CRYSTAL PALACE, 1851	**1851** Crystal Palace built to house the Great Exhibition, celebrating the "Industry of All Nations," London **1856** Gustave Flaubert (1821–80) completes *Madame Bovary*	**1862** *Les Misérables*, by Victor Hugo (1802–85), published **1865** Lewis Carroll (1832–98) writes *Alice's Adventures in Wonderland* **1869** Suez Canal opens
SCIENCE & INVENTION	**1840** Postage stamps introduced in Britain ➡104 **1842** General anesthetic first used by American surgeon Crawford Long (1815–78) **1845** First pneumatic tires used, Scotland	**1856** First internal combustion engine developed in Italy and set up in Florence railroad station **1859** *The Origin of Species*, by Charles Darwin (1809–82), published	**1862** First plastic invented by Alexander Parkes (1813–90) **1865** Antiseptic surgery first practiced by Joseph Lister (1827–1912) ➡105 **1866** Dynamite invented by Alfred Nobel (1833–96)

1870	1880	1890

1870–71 Franco–Prussian War: France defeated

1871 Britain legalizes trade unions

1871 Otto von Bismarck (1815–98) unites German Empire ➡108

1872 Samurai's feudal control in Japan ends

1876 Battle of Little Bighorn: Native Americans defeat US army

1879 Zulu War: British defeat Zulus, South Africa

1881 First Boer War: Boers rebel against British rule, South Africa

1883 Volcano erupts on island of Krakatoa, Java

1884 Berlin Conference decides colonial divisions in Africa ➡109

1885 Indian National Congress Party founded

1886 Gold discovered in South Africa

ZULU WARRIOR, 1879

1890 Battle of Wounded Knee: last massacre of Native Americans in US

1893 New Zealand becomes first country to give women the vote

1894–95 Chinese–Japanese War: Japanese are victorious and occupy Korea

1895–96 Italy and Ethiopia at war: Ethiopia wins

1898 Spanish–American War: US victorious

1899 Boxer rebellion of Chinese peasants

1899–1902 Second Boer War: Britain wins control of South Africa

---

1874 First exhibition of Impressionist painters, including Claude Monet (1840–1926), Paris, France

1874 Paris Opera House completed, France

1876 Mark Twain (1835–1910) writes *Tom Sawyer*

1884 First skyscraper, 10 floors high, is built in Chicago

1886 Statue of Liberty unveiled in New York Harbor

1889 Eiffel Tower built, Paris, France

EIFFEL TOWER, 1889

1891 *Tess of the D'Urbervilles*, by Thomas Hardy (1840–1928) published

1894 Rudyard Kipling (1865–1936) writes *The Jungle Book*

1895 Art Nouveau style of decoration becomes fashionable

1876 Telephone invented by Alexander Graham Bell (1847–1922)

1879 Light bulb invented, England and US

1884 First underground railroad opens, London, England

1885 Louis Pasteur (1822–95) produces vaccine against rabies

1885 Automobile invented by Karl Benz (1844–1929)

1895 Motion pictures shown in public for the first time by inventors Auguste (1862–1954) and Louis (1864–1948) Lumière

1895 Wireless telegraph invented by Guglielmo Marconi (1874–1937)

THE AGE OF REASON

IN A MOVEMENT KNOWN as the Enlightenment, scientists and philosophers began to challenge accepted beliefs. They put forward new ideas about justice and liberty, which inspired later political revolutions.

NEWTON'S TELESCOPE, 1668

ENLIGHTENMENT FIGURES

NAME	DATES	INFORMATION
Isaac Newton	1642–1727	British scientist who worked out the law of gravity and discovered that white light is made up of many colors.
Voltaire	1694–1778	French writer who criticized governments and churchmen for their rigid thinking. He was imprisoned twice for his radical writings.
Carolus Linnaeus	1707–1778	Swedish naturalist who devised a way of classifying plants according to their shared features, a system still used today.
Denis Diderot	1713–1784	French writer who helped to compile the first encyclopedia, which collected many Enlightenment ideas.

AGRICULTURAL CHANGES
In the 18th century, farmers began to create new strains of livestock and used crop rotation to preserve soil quality.

Basic tools like this changed little during the 18th century

HORSE-DRAWN PLOW, 1763

Coulter cuts vertically through the soil

SCIENCE

Enlightenment thinkers believed the key to understanding the world was science, rather than religion. Scientists relied on new methods of careful observation and experimentation. They made great advances and came up with many discoveries, from steam engines to vaccination against disease, from hot-air balloons to lightning conductors.

Sliding focus

ENLIGHTENMENT BOOKS

• *The Social Contract* by French writer Jean-Jacques Rousseau (1712–78) inspired revolutionaries in France and America.

• The writings of French philosopher Montesquieu (1689–1755) influenced new constitutions such as the United States Constitution.

COOK'S VOYAGES

THE SOUTH SEAS

British navigator Captain James Cook (1728–79) made three voyages to Australia, New Zealand, and many South Pacific islands. Cook looked after his crews well, keeping them healthy by giving them fresh vegetables and fresh lime juice to ward off scurvy.

LIMES

Used to work out position at sea

SCIENCE AT SEA

Cook took a scientific approach to exploration. Scientists on Cook's voyages surveyed the coasts and investigated local plants and wildlife.

SEXTANT

COOK MEETS PACIFIC ISLANDERS

THE AMERICAN REVOLUTION

DURING THE 1760s, the British government began to tax North American colonists, even though the colonists were given no representation in the British Parliament. The colonists refused to pay, and war broke out in 1775. In 1783, the colonists defeated the British and won their independence.

STARS AND STRIPES
The first American flag had 13 stars and 13 stripes for the 13 original states.

REVOLUTIONARY LEADERS

NAME	DATES	INFORMATION
George Washington	1732–1799	Army commander who was elected first President of the United States in 1789.
Thomas Jefferson	1743–1826	Helped to draft the Declaration of Independence; became third President.
Benjamin Franklin	1706–1790	Negotiated peace with Britain; helped to draft the Constitution.

CROSSING
THE DELAWARE
On Christmas night 1776, Washington made a daring crossing of the Delaware River, taking the British by surprise.

Washington

American flag

9 8

IMPORTANT BATTLES

• In 1775, the Americans won the war's first battle, at Lexington.

• In 1777, British forces surrendered at Saratoga.

• In 1781, the British surrendered at Yorktown, leading to the end of the war.

Cocked hat

British soldiers were known as redcoats

Most colonists wore blue coats

Musket

THE AMERICANS
With poor organization, the Americans sometimes found it difficult to supply their troops. However, they knew the local terrain and could get reinforcements easily.

THE BRITISH
Some British leaders moved their troops deliberately slowly, because they wanted a political solution to the war.

CONSTITUTION
Under the new Constitution, the federal government had clear power. A Bill of Rights and other systems maintained balanced power and protected individual rights, such as freedom of speech and trial by jury.

TOUSSAINT L'OUVERTURE
In 1791, the slaves of the Caribbean island of Sainte Domingue (Haiti) organized a rebellion, led by Pierre Toussaint l'Ouverture (1743–1803), a former slave. The revolutionaries made Toussaint governor of the island. Eventually, Toussaint was captured by Napoleon, who reintroduced slavery.

TOUSSAINT L'OUVERTURE

THE FRENCH REVOLUTION

THE PEOPLE OF 18TH-CENTURY FRANCE had long suffered from high taxes, bad harvests, and limitations on their freedom. On July 14, 1789, an angry crowd stormed the Bastille prison in Paris, starting the French Revolution.

LOUIS XVI
After trying to make concessions to the people, King Louis XVI (b.1754) was executed in January 1793.

Guillotine

MARIE ANTOINETTE
Hated because of her lavish lifestyle, the queen (b.1755) was executed in October 1793.

THE TERROR
During the Reign of Terror, opponents of revolutionary leader Maximilien Robespierre (1758–94) were ruthlessly guillotined. Robespierre himself was executed in 1794.

New French flag

Basket for bodies

Crowd watching executions

Napoleon

A brilliant general in the revolutionary
wars, Napoleon Bonaparte (1769–1821)
wanted to rule France himself. In 1804,
he made himself Emperor and then
launched a series of ambitious
military campaigns to conquer
much of Europe.

NAPOLEONIC WARS

By 1809, Napoleon had
conquered most of Europe.
However, the British defeated
him at Trafalgar in 1805, and
his 1812 Russian campaign ended in a disastrous
retreat with many French troops losing their lives.

NAPOLEON'S ARMY

The army was
run with great
efficiency. Promotion
was according to
ability, rather than
money or family
connections. Troops
were usually well
provided with food
and other supplies.

THE NAPOLEONIC CODE

A new legal system was
set up, which is still the
basis of French law.
The code included:

• Freedom of religion.

• Equality for all before
the law.

• Abolition of class
privileges.

Borodino, 1812

Waterloo, 1815

Jena, 1806

Austerlitz, 1805

FRENCH EMPIRE

To Spain and Portugal 1808

Marengo 1800

Trafalgar, 1805

To Egypt, 1798

BATTLES AND CAMPAIGNS

In 1815, the combined efforts of the Prussians and
British at Waterloo, Belgium, finally brought about
Napoleon's final defeat. Napoleon was exiled to the
South Atlantic island of St. Helena, where he died.

UNREST AND UPRISINGS

THE FIRST HALF of the 19th century saw uprisings and revolutions in many countries. In Europe, people rose up against oppressive regimes, while in South America, the struggle for independence began.

Europe

KARL MARX
German writer
Karl Marx
(1818–83) pressed
for social reforms.

Bad harvests, famine, unemployment, and economic depression made many people discontented in Europe in the 1840s, and they began to rise up against the governments in power. Most of the revolutions were defeated, but in many cases the rulers had to make some concessions to the people, such as granting constitutions.

Prussian soldier

PRUSSIAN REVOLT
The Prussian uprising led to rebellions in other German-speaking states and pressure for a united Germany.

1848 – YEAR OF REVOLUTIONS	
AREA	EVENTS
France	Workers and middle classes bring down King Louis Philippe (1773–1848).
Prussia	Uprising is quelled by King Frederick William IV (1795–1861); constitution is granted.
Austria	Revolution forces Prince Metternich (1773–1859) to flee to London.
Italian states	Sicilian revolt spreads north, forcing Austrians out of Italy and Pope into temporary exile.
Hungary	Uprising against Austrian rule crushed with the help of Russian forces.

FAMINE AND EMIGRATION
In Ireland in 1846, a disease destroyed the potato crop. Over a million people who relied upon potatoes as a staple food died of starvation. As a result, many people decided to emigrate to North America. Many German people also left for the US at this time.

South America

Spain and Portugal had ruled over much of South America for 150 years. Encouraged by the American and French Revolutions, South American nations began to seek self-government in the early 19th century. The new nations created in this period have survived to the present day.

INDEPENDENCE LEADERS
• Simon Bolivar (1783–1830) helped many countries to independence and hoped to unite all of South America.
• José de San Martin (1778–1850) led uprisings in Argentina, Peru, and Chile.

VENEZUELA 1821
COLOMBIA 1819   GUIANA
PERU 1821   BRAZIL (Portuguese) 1822
BOLIVIA 1825
URUGUAY 1828
CHILE 1818   ARGENTINA 1816

INDEPENDENCE

SPANISH COLONIES (WITH INDEPENDENCE DATES)

DUTCH, FRENCH, AND BRITISH COLONIES

LIBERATION
As in many other South American states, it took several attempts before the Spanish were expelled from Chile. Finally, in 1818, people danced under their new national flag.

THE INDUSTRIAL REVOLUTION

IN THE 19TH CENTURY, new technology began to transform the way people worked and lived their lives. Better transportation, new cities, and large factories with machines powered by water wheels or steam engines began to appear. This industrial revolution began in Britain, but soon spread across Europe and to the US.

PENNY POST
The first stamps were used in Britain in 1840.

Train transporting materials

Railroad bridge

Factory

Canal barge

Small houses for workers

A NEW WAY OF LIFE
Huge numbers of people began to move away from the countryside and into the towns so that they could find work in the new factories.

INDUSTRIAL REVOLUTION INNOVATIONS

STEAM LOCOMOTIVE, 1814

Piston

Tender for coal and water

STEAM ENGINES AND RAILROADS
The steam engine was developed in the 18th century to pump water out of mines and to power factory machinery. In the early 19th century, steam engines were first used to power railroad trains, and a new era of transportation had begun. Soon, steam-powered trains were hauling both goods and passengers.

MEDICAL ADVANCES
There were many developments in medicine, from the use of ether as an anesthetic, to the invention of the stethoscope. Antiseptics helped to reduce the risk of infections that had previously been a common cause of death after surgery.

Mouthpiece

ETHER INHALER, 1847

Sponges soaked in ether

COIL FROM FARADAY'S TRANSFORMER

ELECTRICITY
In 1821, British scientist Michael Faraday (1791–1867) invented the electric motor, but electricity was not commonly used in the home until the 20th century.

INDUSTRIAL MACHINERY
One of the first businesses to use machines on a large scale was the textile industry. In the past, spinning and weaving had been done on small machines in people's homes. Large steam-powered machines had to be housed in factories, and so textile workers now had to go out to work.

SPINNING FRAME, 1769

Bobbin holding yarn

THE AMERICAN CIVIL WAR

IN 1861, WAR BROKE OUT between the northern and southern states of the US. The South feared the growing economic power of the industrial North, and resented its efforts to ban slavery. The war lasted until the South surrendered in 1865.

The Confederate uniform was gray or oatmeal-colored

Union soldiers wore blue uniforms

UNION STATES

SLAVE STATES STILL IN THE UNION

CONFEDERATE STATES

A COUNTRY DIVIDED
Eleven southern states broke away from the Union to form the Confederacy. Five slave states remained in the Union.

THE SOUTH	THE NORTH
• The South's total population was about 9 million.	• The North's total population was about 22 million.
• The Confederate army numbered 850,000 men.	• The Union army numbered 2,100,000 men.
• There were about 260,000 deaths.	• There were about 360,000 deaths.

NATIVE AMERICANS

From the mid-19th century, settlers began to farm on the plains of North America. They killed the buffalo and cleared land, threatening the lifestyle of Native Americans who had lived there for thousands of years. The Native Americans fought back, and many were killed. Those who were left were forced to live on reservations, where they settled down to farm or faced poverty and unemployment.

Hide bag

WARRIOR'S BOW
AND ARROWS

SIOUX
WARRIORS

FLAG OF THE CONFEDERACY

After the North won the war, there were many reforms in the South. Slavery was abolished, free schooling was introduced, and taxes were made fairer.

A MODERN WAR

In many ways, the Civil War was the first modern war. Railroads and iron ships were used to transport troops, field telegraphs relayed messages from commanders, and newspaper reporters sent back reports and photographs from the battlefields.

GLASS-PLATE CAMERA, 1860S

INSTRUMENT CASE OF
MILITARY SURGEON, 1860S

NEW NATIONS

IN THE 19TH CENTURY, the maps of Africa and Europe began to take their modern shape. Italy and Germany became nations in their own right, and European powers began to carve up Africa.

Italy and Germany

Sardinian King Victor Emmanuel II (1820–78) drove the Austrians out of Italy, and united all of Italy except Venice and Rome in 1860. German unification centered around Prussia, under the leadership of King William I (1797–1888).

ITALIAN NATIONAL FLAG
WITH THE ARMS OF SAVOY

GARIBALDI
Revolutionary leader Giuseppe Garibaldi (1807–82) conquered Sicily and united southern Italy with the north.

THE NEW GERMANY

• Germany was made up of 38 states before unification in 1871.

• By 1914, Germany's army was 12 times the size of the British army.

• Germany built up a university system that trained some of the world's best scientists and engineers.

Eagle, the symbol of Prussia

PRUSSIAN MIGHT
Under Chancellor Otto von Bismarck (1815–98), Prussia became one of the strongest powers in Europe and was able to dominate the other German states. In 1871, King William was proclaimed Emperor of Germany.

GERMAN HELMET, EARLY 20TH CENTURY

The scramble for Africa

In the last 30 years of the 19th century, European powers competed in taking over vast territories in Africa. They wanted cheap African raw materials for industries at home. In 1884, European leaders held a conference in Berlin to agree on their claims to African land.

COCOA
Tropical regions of Africa proved a good environment for growing cocoa.

AFRICA DIVIDED

- FRENCH
- BRITISH
- GERMAN
- PORTUGUESE
- BELGIAN
- SPANISH
- ITALIAN
- ANGLO-EGYPTIAN CONDOMINIUM

COTTON
In the late 19th century, cotton was a vital raw material for expanding European textile mills.

Diamond

DIAMONDS AND GOLD
The search for wealth in the form of gold and diamonds attracted many European adventurers to Africa.

COFFEE
Plantations were set up all over southern and central Africa, producing coffee for export to Europe.

1900 TO 1990s

TIME CHART

	1900	1905	1910
EVENTS	**1900** Expansion of German navy begins arms race with Britain **1901** Commonwealth of Australia proclaimed **1901** Peace of Peking ends Boxer Rebellion in China **1903** First Tour de France bicycle race **1903** Votes for Women Movement formed in Britain by Emmeline Pankhurst (1858–1928) **1904** Entente Cordiale (friendly understanding) between Britain and France **1904–5** Russo–Japanese War: Japan victorious	**1905** Union of South Africa formed from former Boer republics **1905** Workers' uprising put down by imperial troops, Russia **1905** World's largest diamond found, South Africa **1906** Earthquake hits San Francisco, California **1907** Oil discovered, Iran **1909** Robert Peary (1856–1920) claims to have reached the North Pole	AMUNDSEN AT SOUTH POLE, 1911 **1911** Chinese revolution overthrows Manchu dynasty **1911** Roald Amundsen (1872–1928) reaches South Pole **1912** African National Congress formed ➡121 **1912–13** Balkan Wars: Greece, Serbia, Bulgaria, and Montenegro against Turkey **1914–18** World War I ➡118, 119
ARTS & ARCHITECTURE	**1903** *The Call of the Wild,* by Jack London (1876–1916), published **1904** Giacomo Puccini (1858–1924) writes *Madame Butterfly* SIGMUND FREUD	**1907** First comic strips appear in US **1907** Pablo Picasso (1881–1973) leads Cubist movement in art **1908** First steel and glass building, AEG factory, Berlin	**1910** Paul Klee (1879–1940) pioneers abstract art movement **1913** Premiere of *The Rites of Spring* by Igor Stravinsky (1882–1971) causes riot in theater **1914** Panama Canal opens
SCIENCE & INVENTION	**1900** *The Interpretation of Dreams,* by Sigmund Freud (1856–1939), published **1903** Orville (1871–1948) and Wilbur (1867–1912) Wright make the first powered flight, US	**1905** Albert Einstein (1879–1955) develops his Special Theory of Relativity **1909** Chromosomes established as carriers of heredity	**1911** Cellophane first manufactured **1911** Ernest Rutherford (1871–1937) announces nuclear theory that the atom contains a central nucleus **1914** Zippers go on sale

1915	1920	1925
1915 Mohandas K. Gandhi (1869–1948) becomes leader of Indian National Congress Party ➡121 **1916** Easter Rising against British rule, Ireland ➡121 **1917** Revolt against French rule, Chad **1917** Russian Revolution ➡120, 121 **1918** Women gain vote in Britain **1918–21** Russian Civil War: Bolsheviks defeat anticommunists	**1920** Women gain vote in US **1920–33** Prohibition of sale of alcohol in US **1922** Discovery of tomb of Tutankhamun, Egypt **1922** Egypt wins independence from Britain **1923** Ireland wins partial independence from Britain ➡121 **1924** Josef Stalin (1879–1953) becomes leader of USSR TUTANKHAMEN'S TOMB FOUND, 1922	**1926** In Britain, a general strike almost brings the country to a standstill; it is defeated by police and army **1928** Mao Tse-tung (1893–1976) and Communists attempt to overthrow Chinese government led by Chiang Kai-shek (1887–1975) ➡124 **1929** Arabs attack Jews in Palestine in a conflict over use of the Wailing Wall, Jerusalem **1929** Leon Trotsky (1879–1940) exiled from USSR **1929** US stock market crashes ➡122
1915 *The Tramp*, starring Charlie Chaplin (1889–1977), wins international acclaim **1919** Bauhaus school of architecture and design founded in Germany	**1922** Completion of earthquake-proof hotel, Tokyo, designed by Frank Lloyd Wright (1867–1959) **1922** *The Waste Land*, by T. S. Eliot (1888–1965), published	**1927** Stan Laurel (1890–1965) and Oliver Hardy (1892–1957) make the first of several films together **1927** *The Jazz Singer*, the first "talkie" (feature film with sound), is released LAUREL AND HARDY
1915 First transcontinental telephone call **1915** Tractors introduced by Ford **1916** Tanks invented by William Tritton (1875–1946) as a British secret weapon	**1920** Regular radio broadcasting begins in US **1922** Insulin first used for the treatment of diabetes **1924** Clarence Birdseye (1886–1956) experiments with quick-frozen foods	**1928** First TV broadcasts **1928** Jet engine invented by Frank Whittle (b.1907) **1928** Penicillium mold discovered by Alexander Fleming (1881–1955), leading to invention of antibiotics (1940)

Time Chart

	1930	1935	1940
EVENTS	**1930** Ras Tafari (1892–1975) is crowned Haile Selassie in Ethiopia ➡125 **1931** Canada gains full independence from Britain **1931–33** Chinese–Japanese War: Japan victorious **1933** Adolf Hitler (1889–1945) becomes German Chancellor ➡125 **1934–35** Long March in China ➡124	**1935** Italy invades Ethiopia ➡125 **1936** Germany hosts Olympic Games in Berlin **1936** Italy signs alliance with Germany ➡125 **1936–39** Spanish Civil War ➡124 **1937** Japan and China at war **1938** Germany takes over Czechoslovakia ➡125 **1939** Germany invades Poland **1939–45** World War II ➡126, 127	**1940** Germany occupies Denmark, Norway, France, Belgium, and the Netherlands **1941** Allied troops overrun Italy's African colonies **1941** Germans move into eastern Europe **1941** Japanese planes attack US fleet at Pearl Harbor ➡126 **1941–42** Japan takes over American, British, and Dutch colonies in Indian and Pacific Oceans ➡127 **1944** Allies invade France and drive back Germans
ARTS & ARCHITECTURE	**1930** Salvador Dali (1904–84) pioneers the Surrealist movement in art **1930** The opera *The Rise and Fall of the City of Mahagonny* by Kurt Weill (1900–50) is performed **1931** Empire State Building built, New York	**1935** Musical theater reaches its peak with first performance of *Porgy and Bess* by George Gershwin (1898–1937) **1936** Hoover Dam completed, US ➡123	**1940** *Darkness at Noon* by Arthur Koestler (1905–83) describes life under Stalinism **1940** Duke Ellington (1899–1974) becomes popular as jazz pianist and composer
SCIENCE & INVENTION	**1931** Electron microscope invented by Ernst Ruska (1906–88) **1933–35** Radar invented in Britain and Germany **1934** Wallace Carothers (1896–1937) invents nylon	**1939** DDT insecticide first used to kill mosquitoes **1939** Igor Sikorsky (1889–1972) invents single rotor helicopter **1939** Jet aircraft built by Ernst Heinkel (1888–1958)	**1941** First aerosol cans **1942** Enrico Fermi (1901–54) builds first nuclear reactor, US **1942** Rocket-propelled missile invented by Wernher von Braun (1912–77)

WORLD WAR II AIRPLANES, 1939–45

1 1 4

1945	1950	1955

1945 German forces surrender

1945 US drops atomic bombs on Hiroshima and Nagasaki ➡127

1947 India wins independence from Britain ➡132

1948 State of Israel created ➡136

1949 Germany split into East and West ➡128

1949 Mao proclaims new Communist Republic of China

1949 NATO formed ➡130

ATOM BOMB, 1945

1950 China occupies Tibet

1950 Group Area Act legalizes apartheid, South Africa

1950 US Senator Joseph McCarthy (1908–57) begins anticommunist "witch-hunts"

1950–53 Korean War ➡131

1953 Tensing Norgay (1914–86) and Edmund Hillary (b.1919) are the first to climb Mount Everest, the world's highest mountain

1955 Black people in Montgomery, Alabama, boycott segregated buses

1955 Warsaw Pact formed ➡130

1956 Hungarian uprising

1956 Suez Crisis: Egyptian troops force French and British to withdraw

1957 European Economic Community formed ➡129

1957 Pass Laws in South Africa state that all nonwhites must carry passes

1959 Revolution in Cuba brings Fidel Castro (b.1927) to power

---

1945 Abstract Expressionist style of art develops in US, led by Jackson Pollock (1912–56)

1946 Jean Paul Sartre (1905–80), pioneer of the Existentialist movement, writes *Being and Nothingness*

ELVIS PRESLEY

1950 Theater of the Absurd developed by Samuel Beckett (1906–89) and Eugène Ionesco (1912–94)

1956 Rock and roll music reaches height of popularity with artists such as Elvis Presley (1935–77)

1957 Boris Pasternak (1890–1960) writes *Doctor Zhivago*

1945 First electronic computer developed

1947 Sound barrier first broken by Bell XI aircraft

1948 Invention of the transistor makes it possible to build smaller electronic equipment

1953 Link between smoking and lung cancer established

1953 Structure of DNA discovered

1953–5 Polio vaccine developed

1954 Hydrogen bomb tested by the US

1955 Tefal company develops nonstick pans, France

1957 USSR launches first artificial satellite ➡131

1958 Integrated circuit, or "silicon chip," invented

TIME CHART

	. 1960	1966	1972
EVENTS	**1960** 17 African colonies gain independence ➡133 **1961** Berlin Wall built **1963** President John F. Kennedy (b.1917) is assassinated **1964** ANC leader Nelson Mandela (b.1918) is jailed in South Africa ➡133 **1965** Civil rights leader Malcolm X (b.1925) is assassinated ➡134 **1965–75** Vietnam War ➡131	MARTIN LUTHER KING, JR. **1966** Cultural Revolution begins in China ➡135 **1967** Six Day War between Israelis and Arabs ➡137 **1968** Anticommunist uprising in Prague crushed ➡134 **1968** Civil rights leader Martin Luther King, Jr. (b.1929) is assassinated ➡134 **1968** Civil war begins in Northern Ireland **1968** Student riots in Paris	**1972** Independent state of Bangladesh created **1973** Arab–Israeli War ➡137 **1974** President Richard Nixon (1913–95) resigns over Watergate scandal **1975** Juan Carlos (b.1938) becomes Spanish King after death of Francisco Franco (b.1892) **1976** North and South Vietnam reunited after 22 years of separation **1976** Riots in black townships across South Africa
ARTS & ARCHITECTURE	**1960** Pop Art pioneered by Roy Lichtenstein (b.1923) and Andy Warhol (1928–87) in US **1962** British pop group The Beatles have their first hit, *Love Me Do*	**1967** Gabriel García Márquez (b.1928) writes *One Hundred Years of Solitude*	**1972** Sydney Opera House opened, Australia **1976** Punk rock emerges in England, led by British group, the Sex Pistols **1977** Pompidou Center completed, Paris SYDNEY OPERA HOUSE, 1972
SCIENCE & INVENTION	**1960** Laser invented for use in precision cutting and surgery, US **1961** Yuri Gagarin (1934–68) is first man in space ➡131 **1965** Space probe sends back first pictures from Mars	**1967** Christiaan Barnard (b.1922) performs first heart transplant **1969** Concorde becomes the first supersonic passenger aircraft **1969** First moon landing ➡131	**1973** Videotex (text transmission via television) is developed **1975** Soviet and American spacecraft link up in space **1975** Video recorder launched by Sony Corporation

1 1 6

1978

1978 Margaret Thatcher (b.1925) becomes Britain's first woman prime minister

1979 Camp David peace treaty between Egypt and Israel ➡137

1979 Iranian Revolution

1979 Marxist Sandinistas take power in Nicaragua

1980 Lech Walesa (b.1943) leads Solidarity trade union in Poland

1980–88 Iran–Iraq War ➡133

1982 Falklands War: Britain defeats Argentine forces

1983 Famine in Ethiopia

1984

1984 New Zealand declared a nuclear-free zone

1989 Chinese security forces put down prodemocracy movement in Beijing's Tiananmen Square

1989 Communist governments overthrown in eastern Europe ➡138

1989 Martial law imposed in Lhasa, Tibet, by Chinese

FAMINE IN ETHIOPIA, 1983

1990

1990 Gulf War begins ➡137

1990 Namibia gains independence from South Africa

1991 Break-up of Soviet Union ➡138

1992 Civil war begins, former Yugoslavia

1992 Muslim–Hindu riots, India

1994 ANC wins South Africa's first free elections

1994 IRA ceasefire begins in Northern Ireland

1994 PLO gains autonomy in Gaza strip

1978 AT&T Building, New York, by Philip Johnson (b.1906), and Portland Building, Oregon, by Michael Graves (b.1934), pioneer the style of postmodernism

1978 Disco music and dancing become popular

1986 Hong Kong and Shanghai Bank, Hong Kong, opens, designed by Norman Foster (b.1935)

1994 Channel Tunnel between England and France opened

1995 Artist Christo (b.1935) wraps German Reichstag building in silver fabric

---

1978 First "test-tube" baby born, England ➡139

1980 Smallpox is eradicated

1981 First reuseable space shuttle launched in US

1981 Solar-powered aircraft crosses English Channel

1984 French and American scientists identify AIDS-related HIV virus

1984 Genetic fingerprinting, a technique for identifying people by their unique DNA pattern, is pioneered

1990s Computers all over the world are linked via telephone lines to create the Internet

1990s Interactive CD-ROMs are introduced

1995 American space shuttle Challenger docks with Russian space station Mir

WORLD WAR I

IN JULY 1914, war broke out between Serbia and Austria after a Serbian nationalist murdered the heir to the Austrian throne. Most European powers had an alliance with one of the two sides, so they were soon drawn into the crisis. The Great War grew to a scale never seen before. By 1918, the death toll had reached 20 million.

INFANTRYMAN
Most of the fighting was done on the ground, by men like this French soldier.

A NEW KIND OF WAR

The war was very different from previous conflicts. It involved the whole adult populations of many nations. Large numbers of men were called up to fight, while women took over men's jobs or worked in armaments factories. Poison gas and tanks were used for the first time, and airplanes were used for observation, bombing, and fighting.

Propeller   Top wing

Observer seat

BE 2B
BOMBER, 1914

National marking

687

WORLD WAR I BATTLES	
BATTLE	INFORMATION
Tannenberg, August 1914	Germans halt the advance of the Russians, taking some 125,000 men prisoner.
The Marne, September 1914	Last mobile action of the war in the west; French and British push back the Germans.
Gallipoli, April 1915	Australia, New Zealand, and Britain suffer many casualties trying to take Constantinople.
Passchendaele, July 1917	British and Canadians make a small advance, but at the cost of more than 250,000 lives.
Cambrai, November 1917	British tanks break through German lines, causing a German collapse.

Sandbags Wooden props Barbed wire

German troops run into No-Man's Land

TRENCH WARFARE
Much of the war in northern Europe was fought between parallel lines of trenches. Soldiers were ordered to charge into the area of No-Man's Land between the trenches to push back the enemy.

CENTRAL POWERS
ALLIES
NEUTRAL NATIONS

PORTUGAL · SPAIN · BRITAIN · BELGIUM · GERMANY · FRANCE · ITALY · RUSSIA · AUSTRO-HUNGARIAN EMPIRE · ROMANIA · BULGARIA · SERBIA · GREECE · OTTOMAN EMPIRE

THE HUMAN COST
About 4.9 million Allied troops died in battle and 113 million were wounded. The Central Powers lost 3.1 million troops in battle and 8.4 million were wounded.

500,000 German
400,000 British
200,000 French
BATTLE OF THE SOMME CASUALTIES

WESTERN FRONTS
Countries that fought with Germany and Austria were known as the Central Powers; their opponents became known as the Allies. The US entered the war on the Allied side at the end of 1917.

REVOLUTION AND RESISTANCE

LOW PAY IN THE CITIES, poor conditions for farmers, and the Czar's tyrannical rule led to discontent in early 20th-century Russia. Workers began to demand their rights, and in 1917, revolution erupted. By the end of the year, the Soviet Union, the world's first communist nation, had been founded.

Pictures of the royal family

THE CZAR AND HIS FAMILY
Nicholas II (1868–1918) was forced to abdicate in 1917. He and his family were shot dead by the Bolsheviks in 1918.

Inlaid with precious stones

RED AND WHITE

• Known as the Reds, the Communist Bolsheviks were led by Vladimir Lenin (1870–1924).

• After the revolution, anti-Bolshevists became known as White Russians.

ROYAL RICHES
Palaces filled with art treasures made a stark contrast with the living conditions of the poor. These conditions worsened dramatically following crushing Russian defeats in World War I.

EGG MADE BY ROYAL JEWELER FABERGÉ

Winter Palace

Cruiser Aurora fires blanks at the palace

Communist hammer and sickle symbol

THE NEW REGIME

The communists gave more land to peasants and gave workers control of their factories.

SIEGE OF THE WINTER PALACE

After the Czar abdicated, a temporary government was set up. But discontent continued and in October 1917, the Bolsheviks besieged the government in the Winter Palace in St Petersburg. Faced by little opposition, the Bolsheviks took power.

RESISTANCE MOVEMENTS AROUND THE WORLD		
PLACE	DATE	INFORMATION
South Africa	1912	The white minority took over most of the land in South Africa, and restricted the rights of nonwhite South Africans. In 1912, the African National Congress (ANC) was founded to defend the rights of black and colored people
Ireland	1916–1922	Britain had promised the Irish Home Rule, but it was delayed because of World War I. Irish nationalists took over Dublin in the Easter Rising, but Britain defeated the rebels. The Irish Free State was finally created in southern Ireland in 1922.
India	1919–1947	The campaign for independence in India led to strikes and riots. After British soldiers massacred more than 300 protesters at Amritsar in 1919, nationalist leader Mohandas K. Gandhi (1869–1948) began his campaign of passive resistance to British rule.

THE GREAT DEPRESSION

THE NEW YORK Stock Exchange
crashed dramatically in October
1929, as shareholders panicked and
sold their shares. Many people lost
their jobs, their savings, their
businesses, and even their homes.
Meanwhile, there was a slump in
agriculture, as overproduction led to
falling prices. The economic crisis
spread to most parts of the world,
causing poverty for millions.

THE DUST BOWL
In the west and midwest
of the US, many farmers
were forced to abandon
their land because low
rainfall made the soil turn
to barren dust.

POVERTY AND HUNGER
The problem of unemployment was
severe in the large cities of the US.
Even before the Stock Market
crash, many businesses
had already failed due
to overpriced shares
and overproduction.
Particularly badly hit
were the mining,
railroad, and textile
industries. As a
result, thousands of
families could no
longer afford to eat.

*Lining up to receive
free food*

THE SOVIET UNION

Soviet leader Josef Stalin (1879–1953) introduced his Five Year Plan to force expansion in industry and agriculture.

• Peasants who objected to giving their lands to the State were imprisoned or killed.

• In spite of the industrial expansion, economic chaos, famine, and poverty were widespread in the early 1930s.

HOOVER DAM, 1936

THE NEW DEAL

New American President Franklin D. Roosevelt (1882–1945) tackled the Depression with a policy known as the New Deal. This included a program of public works, such as forest planting and hydroelectric schemes, designed to get unemployed people back to work.

EUROPE

Europe was badly hit by the Depression.

• There was a sharp fall in industrial production, and trade fell to 35 percent of its 1929 rate.

• Currencies declined in value and prices in the shops rose.

THE MOVIES

The film industry was one of the few businesses that flourished during the Depression years. The new talkies provided people with a cheap distraction from their troubles.

TECHNICOLOR MOVIE CAMERA

Dolly

200,000,000 German Mark note

MAD MONEY

Rising prices made currencies such as the German Mark virtually worthless. At Tenino, Washington, a shortage of cash led to wooden banknotes.

POLITICAL EXTREMES

IN MANY COUNTRIES, governments were blamed for the hardships of the Depression. New strong governments led by dictators dealt successfully with the economic problems, but their extreme beliefs and repressive regimes led to terrible suffering, and ultimately to war.

SPANISH CIVIL WAR
In 1936, Francisco Franco (1892–1975) led a rebellion against the government. By 1939, the government and its communist supporters were defeated. Franco ruled Spain until his death.

Communism

In a communist system, profit-seeking and speculation do not exist, so in theory there can be no economic crises. Under Stalin, industry flourished in the Soviet Union, while in China, the Communists led by Mao Tse-tung (1893–1976) struggled to take power.

The marchers had to make their way over steep mountains and through rocky gorges

THE LONG MARCH
Expelled by the ruling Kuomintang party, Mao and his allies marched 6,000 miles (9,700 km) to set up Communist headquarters in safety. Mao finally took control of China in 1949.

Over three-quarters of the marchers died on the way

Fascism

The fascist governments of Italy and Germany were opposed to democracy. They were led by dictators who took total control and ruthlessly suppressed opposition. Both regimes were eager to expand their power abroad. In 1935, Italy invaded Ethiopia. Germany occupied the Rhineland, took over part of Czechoslovakia, and annexed Austria. In 1936, Italy and Germany joined in a formal alliance.

HITLER
In Germany, the Nazi party came to power in 1933 under Adolf Hitler (1889–1945).

Jewish homes and businesses were destroyed

ANTISEMITISM
From 1935, Jews in Germany were deprived of basic rights by law. Eventually, over 6 million Jews were killed.

The Nazi swastika symbol appeared everywhere

PROPAGANDA
The Nazis used film, radio, the arts, and vast political rallies to brainwash people into accepting Nazi beliefs.

MUSSOLINI
Benito Mussolini (1883–1945) came to power in 1922, and by 1925 ruled Italy as a dictator. In 1940, he brought Italy into World War II on Germany's side.

WORLD WAR II

IN 1939, WAR BROKE OUT in Europe
after Germany invaded Poland.
Then, in 1941, Japan attacked the
US Navy base at Pearl Harbor,
Hawaii, bringing the US into
the war. Once again, much of
the world was at war.

BLITZKRIEG
By 1942, with its policy of
"Blitzkrieg" (lightning war),
Germany controlled most
of Europe. The tide turned
in 1943 with Allied
rearmament and the
American
entry into
the war.

EUROPEAN WAR ZONE

The German army seemed
unstoppable as they marched
through Europe.

- AXIS STATES
- CONTROLLED BY AXIS
- ALLIED STATES
- CONTROLLED BY ALLIES
- NEUTRAL STATES

EXTENT OF GERMAN OCCUPATION, 1942

NORWAY   SWEDEN   FINLAND

IRELAND   DENMARK   SOVIET UNION

Atlantic   BRITAIN
Ocean   NETHERLANDS
            BELGIUM
FRANCE   GERMANY
        SWITZERLAND   HUNGARY
                CROATIA
SPAIN   SERBIA   Black Sea
            ITALY   BULGARIA
    MOROCCO   ALBANIA GREECE   TURKEY
                        CYPRUS   SYRIA
ALGERIA   Mediterranean Sea   LEBANON
                    PALESTINE
        LIBYA   EGYPT

1960 1980 1996

SOVIET
UNION

CHINA

KOREA JAPAN

BURMA

MALAYA
PHILIPPINES

Pacific Ocean

DUTCH EAST INDIES

AUSTRALIA

NEW
ZEALAND

☐ AREA CONTROLLED
BY JAPAN, 1942

▬▬ EXTENT OF JAPANESE EXPANSION

THE ARMIES
The Soviets
supported the Axis
states until 1941,
when Germany
invaded the
USSR. In 1941,
Japan entered the
war on the side
of Germany.

GERMAN

JAPANESE ITALIAN

THE WAR IN THE EAST
Japan invaded British, Dutch, and American
colonies in the Pacific. The US finally forced the
Japanese to surrender in 1945 by dropping atomic
bombs on Hiroshima and Nagasaki.

WORLD WAR II BATTLES

BATTLE	DATE	INFORMATION
Battle of Britain	1940	British halt German invasion plans.
Midway	1942	Defeat of Japanese Navy by US.
El Alamein	1942	British push back Germans in Africa.
Stalingrad	1943	German army surrenders to Soviets.
Normandy (D-Day)	1944	Allies invade Normandy, France.

AMERICAN SOVIET BRITISH

The aftermath of war

After the German surrender in May 1945, Germany was initially divided into four zones, each controlled by one of the Allied powers: Britain, France, the Soviet Union, and the US. In 1949, the three western sectors were merged to become West Germany. The Soviet sector became a communist republic, East Germany.

BERLIN AIRLIFT
Berlin in East Germany was also divided into four sectors. In 1948, the USSR blockaded the city, preventing Westerners from bringing in supplies by land. Supplies were brought in by air for five months.

Many unstable buildings were demolished

DESTRUCTION OF CITIES
Many cities had been badly damaged in air raids, and millions of civilians had lost their lives. After the war, cities had to be restored.

Houses had been ripped apart, leaving many people homeless

DEATH TOLL

COUNTRY	DEATHS
US	298,000
Britain	357,000
Italy	395,000
Japan	1,972,000
Germany	4,200,000
Soviet Union	18,000,000

ITALY
BRITAIN
US
JAPAN   GERMANY   SOVIET UNION

NEW INDUSTRY
The industry of Japan and Germany had been badly hit by the war. The West gave economic aid to these countries to help them rebuild their industry.
As Japan and Germany's economies rapidly expanded, they once more became leading industrial powers.

THE EEC
• In 1957, Belgium, France, Italy, Luxembourg, the Netherlands, and West Germany formed the European Economic Community, to remove trade barriers within Europe.

• The organization now has several more members, and is called the European Union. It has its own parliament with representatives from every member.

THE UNITED NATIONS
In 1945, the United Nations (UN) was established with the aim of preventing future wars. The UN promotes human rights, encourages good relations between countries, and tries to find solutions to the world's problems.

THE COLD WAR

AFTER THE WAR, there was a clear split between the democratic West and the communist East. The US and western Europe formed the North Atlantic Treaty Organization (NATO) to defend themselves from possible attack from the USSR and eastern Europe, who formed the Warsaw Pact. The two sides kept an uneasy peace in a situation known as the Cold War.

WEAPONS
Both sides stockpiled and tested conventional and nuclear weapons. They did not actually fight, but conflicts such as the Vietnam War were, in fact, struggles between East and West.

ARMS COMPARISON, 1960							
TROOPS		LONG-RANGE BOMBERS		LAND-BASED MISSILES		SUBMARINES	
US	USSR	USSR	US	US	USSR	US	USSR
2,514,000	3,623,000	190	450	18	35	32	unknown

CONFLICTS AND CRISES

COUNTRY	DATE	INFORMATION
Korea	1950–1953	South Korea, supported by the United Nations, fought North Korea, supported by communist China. VIETNAM WAR HELICOPTERS
Cuba	1962	Communist Cuban leader Fidel Castro (b.1926) allowed the Soviet Union to build missile bases in Cuba. The US blockaded Cuba, forcing the Soviets to remove the bases.
Vietnam	1965–1975	The US, Australia, and New Zealand helped South Vietnam fight communist North Vietnam. In 1973, the Western allies withdrew. North Vietnam won the war in 1975.

The Space Race

In 1957, the Soviet Union surprised the world by launching Sputnik 1, the first artificial satellite. They launched the first manned space flight in 1961. In response, the US stepped up its plans for space exploration. The Space Race was on.

SPUTNIK 1, THE FIRST ARTIFICIAL SATELLITE

THE FINAL FRONTIER
The US organized a space program that led to a manned landing on the Moon in 1969 (right). Meanwhile the Soviets concentrated on unmanned landings and the construction of Earth-orbiting space stations.

INDEPENDENCE MOVEMENTS

AFTER THE WAR, many countries that had been ruled
by European powers gained independence. The new
nations struggled to create their own systems
of government, build up industry and trade,
and cope with internal divisions.
They relied on loans from
richer nations, leading to a
problem of long-term debt.

INDIAN INDEPENDENCE
Britain finally granted
India independence
after World War II.
Indian leaders wanted
to create a united
country for both
Hindus and Muslims,
but most Muslims
preferred to form a
separate state. When
the British left in 1947,
the Muslim country of
Pakistan was created
to the north of the
independent
India.

CELEBRATION
Independence was
often the result of
a long period of
struggle. Huge
celebrations
followed, like this
one in Algeria.

CIVIL WARS
Most new African
states had little unity
because their borders
were based on ones
that had been drawn
up by colonial powers.
As a result, civil wars
often broke out soon
after independence.

AFRICAN INDEPENDENCE

COUNTRY	FLAG	DATE	FORMER RULER	INFORMATION
Ghana		1957	Britain	Corruption and coups dogged Ghana's government after independence.
Congo		1960	France	Independence was followed by civil war, and the Congo's first president was assassinated.
Mauritania		1960	France	The first president was overthrown by a military coup in 1978.
Nigeria		1960	Britain	Nigeria has been under almost constant military rule since independence.
Senegal		1960	France	The country was ruled under a virtual one-party government until the 1980s.
Algeria		1962	France	Independence was negotiated after an armed rebellion and a period of unrest.
Uganda		1962	Britain	A turbulent post-independence period led to over a million deaths.
Kenya		1963	Britain	Kenya was ruled as a one-party state until the first free elections in 1992.
Angola		1975	Portugal	Angola has been in an almost constant state of civil war since 1975.
Mozambique		1975	Portugal	Civil war, debt, and poor food supplies have led to famine and poverty.
Zimbabwe		1980	Britain	The black majority finally defeated the white minority and won independence.

SOUTH AFRICA

For the second half of the 20th century, South
Africa was governed under the apartheid system
which deprived nonwhite people of basic human
rights. The main opposition to apartheid was
organized by the African National Congress
(ANC), which was banned in 1960.
ANC leader Nelson Mandela (b.1918)
was imprisoned from 1964 to 1989.
Following general elections in 1994,
Mandela led the first ANC government.

PROTEST AND CHANGE

THE 1950s AND 1960s saw many groups protesting against discrimination and campaigning for their rights. As a result, many important social changes began in this period, with black people in the US and women in the Western world gaining more rights. This process of change is still continuing today.

MARTIN LUTHER KING

CIVIL RIGHTS
In the US, leaders such as Martin Luther King, Jr., and Malcolm X campaigned for the rights of black people. The lot of black Americans gradually began to improve.

US CIVIL RIGHTS

• In 1964, the Civil Rights Act protected racial minorities.

• The 1965 Voting Rights Act affirmed the right of black Americans to register to vote.

• Malcolm X (b.1925) was assassinated in 1965. King (b.1929) was shot dead in 1968.

Soviet tanks rumbled into Prague in August 1968

The Czech people were powerless

THE PRAGUE SPRING
In 1968, the USSR invaded the Czech capital, Prague. The Soviets were afraid that liberal reforms made by the Czech government might weaken the Warsaw Pact.

Social changes

Many people wanted to transform society in the 1960s. While some groups began to assert their rights, others tried to "drop out" of society, living in peaceful communes, growing food, and sharing their belongings. Many also became worried about the threat of nuclear weapons.

The White House

SEXUAL EQUALITY

The women's movement had four basic demands: equal opportunities in work and education, equal pay, free childcare, and free contraception and abortion.

ELECTORAL RIGHTS

In Western countries today, most adults have the right to vote for the government of their choice. Until the 1990s, a single-party system operated in the communist countries of Eastern Europe, so that even if voting was possible, the choice was severely limited.

THE CULTURAL REVOLUTION

Chinese leader Mao Tse-tung carried out his own Cultural Revolution from 1966. Many universities were closed, and teachers and students were forced to work on the land. Young people were encouraged to join the Red Guards who promoted Mao's policies and attacked those who disagreed.

MIDDLE EAST CRISES

SINCE WORLD WAR II, the Middle East has been one of the world's trouble spots. Disputes between the Jewish state of Israel and her Arab neighbors have dogged the Middle East since Israel was set up in 1948. Millions of Palestinians who used to live in the area are now refugees in other Arab nations. Meanwhile, there have been other conflicts over oil, territory, and religion.

MOSQUE, SUDAN

BLACK GOLD
Oil is the Middle East's most valuable natural resource. Major oil production in the region began in the 1940s, and by the following decade the region was an important producer.

RELIGIOUS STRUGGLES
Judaism, Christianity, and Islam all have their origins in the Middle East. All three consider certain places in Israel, such as Jerusalem, to be important holy sites.

OIL
Control of the world's oil supply has been a major factor in Middle Eastern wars, and has given the area considerable world power.

1959

1945

| 101,156 BARRELS | 1,055,986 BARRELS |

DISPUTED AREAS
This map shows
the main areas
that have been
the scenes of
recent conflicts
in the Middle
East. As well as
disputes over oil
and religious
differences, there
have been many
clashes over
territory in
the region.

| ISRAELI-OCCUPIED TERRITORIES, 1993 | BORDER DISPUTED IN IRAN–IRAQ WAR, 1980–88 | AREA DISPUTED IN GULF WAR, 1991 |

MIDDLE EAST CONFLICTS

WAR	DATE	INFORMATION
Six Day War	1967	Israeli troops seize the West Bank, the Gaza Strip, the Sinai Peninsula, and the Golan Heights, areas which are populated mainly by Palestinians.
Arab–Israeli War	1973	Egypt and Syria attack Israel, and an 18-day war leaves the conflict undecided. Peace treaty finally signed at Camp David, US, 1979.
Iran–Iraq War	1980–1988	Iraqi forces attack the world's largest oil refinery at Abadab, Iran; Iraq gains some territory, but over 1 million people die; a ceasefire is overseen by the UN.
Lebanon	1982	Israel invades Lebanon and lays siege to the capital, Beirut, destroying the power base of the Palestine Liberation Organization (PLO); PLO is forced to evacuate.
West Bank and Gaza	1987–1993	Palestinian uprising in Israeli-occupied territories, but is suppressed by Israel; in 1992, moves toward peace give Palestinians some control over their affairs.
Gulf War	1990–1991	Iraq invades neighboring Kuwait; UN responds by sending troops to fight Iraq; defeated Iraqis set fire to many oil wells as they retreat, causing great environmental damage.

THE WORLD TODAY

THROUGHOUT HISTORY, governments have risen and fallen, and countries have gained or lost power and territory. In recent years, the communist governments of the Soviet Union and Eastern Europe have made way for democratic systems. Some Asian countries have begun to grow in economic importance and world power.

GLASNOST
From 1985, Soviet leader Mikhail Gorbachev (b.1931) began to encourage change within the Soviet Union. His new policies of "Glasnost" (openness) and "Perestroika" (reconstruction) led to the breakup of the USSR.

TORN SOVIET FLAG
The Soviet Union ceased to exist in 1991.

THE COLLAPSE OF COMMUNISM
In 1989, communist governments in Czechoslovakia, Hungary, Romania, and East Germany all fell. The Berlin Wall was taken down in December 1989, paving the way for Germany to be reunited into a single nation.

One world

Today's world seems smaller than it did in the past. Wars concern not just the fighting parties, but also negotiators and peace-keepers from the UN. Crises such as famines involve international aid. Doctors all over the world are searching for cures for diseases such as AIDS. Environmental problems concern the whole planet and must be tackled globally.

CLEAN ENERGY
The world's dependence on fossil fuels such as coal, oil, and gas has caused environmental pollution and even damaged the atmosphere. New, clean energy sources include tidal power, solar power, and wind power.

TODAY'S INNOVATIONS

HOME VIDEO RECORDER
The first video recorders for use at home appeared in the 1970s.

VIDEO RECORDER

COMPUTERS
The early 1980s brought desktop computers that were more powerful than the huge machines of the 1960s and 1970s.

MODERN COMPUTER

TEST-TUBE BABIES
The first baby conceived outside its mother's body was born in 1978.

TEST TUBE AND SYRINGE

THE POWER OF THE PACIFIC RIM
The economies of Hong Kong, Taiwan, Singapore, and South Korea have expanded, learning from Japan's success, and benefiting from low labor costs.

Coelder poort

REFERENCE
SECTION

BRITISH RULERS

THESE LISTS contain the monarchs
of England and Scotland up until
the early 17th century, and the joint
British monarchs from then on.

MONARCHS OF ENGLAND

SAXON
1042–66	Edward the Confessor
1066	Harold II

NORMAN
1066–87	William I, the Conqueror
1087–1100	William II
1100–35	Henry I
1135–54	Stephen

PLANTAGENET
1154–89	Henry II
1189–99	Richard I, the Lionheart
1199–1216	John
1216–72	Henry III
1272–1307	Edward I
1307–27	Edward II
1327–77	Edward III
1377–99	Richard II

LANCASTER
1399–1413	Henry IV
1413–22	Henry V
1422–61	Henry VI

YORK
1461–83	Edward IV
1483	Edward V
1483–85	Richard III

TUDOR
1485–1509	Henry VII
1509–47	Henry VIII
1547–53	Edward VI
1553–58	Mary I
1558–1603	Elizabeth I

MONARCHS OF SCOTLAND

1306–29	Robert I, the Bruce
1329–71	David II

STUART
1371–90	Robert II
1390–1406	Robert III
1406–37	James I
1437–60	James II
1460–88	James III
1488–1513	James IV
1513–42	James V
1542–67	Mary, Queen of Scots
1567–1625	James VI

MONARCHS OF BRITAIN

STUART
1603–25	James I (VI of Scotland)
1625–49	Charles I

1649–60 COMMONWEALTH

STUART
1660–85	Charles II
1685–88	James II
1689–94	Mary II
1689–1702	William III
1702–14	Anne

HANOVER
1714–27	George I
1727–60	George II
1760–1820	George III
1820–30	George IV
1830–37	William IV
1837–1901	Victoria

SAXE-COBURG
1901–10	Edward VII

WINDSOR
1910–36	George V
1936	Edward VIII
1936–52	George VI
1952–	Elizabeth II

BRITISH PRIME MINISTERS

1721–42	Robert Walpole	1858–59	Earl of Derby
1742–43	Earl of Wilmington	1859–65	Viscount Palmerston
1743–54	Henry Pelham	1865–66	Earl Russell
1754–56	Duke of Newcastle	1866–68	Earl of Derby
1756–57	Duke of Devonshire	1868	Benjamin Disraeli
1757–62	Duke of Newcastle	1868–74	William Gladstone
1762–63	Earl of Bute	1874–80	Benjamin Disraeli
1763–65	George Grenville	1880–85	William Gladstone
1765–66	Marquess of Rockingham	1885–86	Marquess of Salisbury
1766–68	Earl of Chatham, Pitt the Elder	1886	William Gladstone
		1886–92	Marquess of Salisbury
1768–70	Duke of Grafton	1892–94	William Gladstone
1770–82	Lord North	1894–95	Earl of Rosebery
1782	Marquess of Rockingham	1895–1902	Marquess of Salisbury
1782–83	Earl of Shelburne	1902–05	Arthur Balfour
1783	Duke of Portland	1905–08	Henry Campbell-Bannerman
1783–1801	William Pitt, the Younger	1908–16	Herbert Asquith
1801–04	Henry Addington	1916–22	David Lloyd-George
1804–06	William Pitt, the Younger	1922–23	Andrew Bonar Law
1806–07	Lord Grenville	1923–24	Stanley Baldwin
1807–09	Duke of Portland	1924	James Ramsay-Macdonald
1809–12	Spencer Perceval	1924–29	Stanley Baldwin
1812–27	Earl of Liverpool	1929–35	James Ramsay-Macdonald
1827	George Canning	1935–37	Stanley Baldwin
1827–28	Viscount Goderich	1937–40	Neville Chamberlain
1828–30	Duke of Wellington	1940–45	Winston Churchill
1830–34	Earl Grey	1945–51	Clement Attlee
1834	Viscount Melbourne	1951–55	Winston Churchill
1834–35	Robert Peel	1955–57	Anthony Eden
1835–41	Viscount Melbourne	1957–63	Harold Macmillan
1841–46	Robert Peel	1963–64	Sir Alec Douglas-Home
1846–52	Lord John Russell	1964–70	Harold Wilson
1852	Earl of Derby	1970–74	Edward Heath
1852–55	Earl of Aberdeen	1974–76	Harold Wilson
1855–58	Viscount Palmerston	1976–79	James Callaghan
		1979–90	Margaret Thatcher
		1990–	John Major

AMERICAN PRESIDENTS

AFTER THE American Revolution, George
Washington became the first President of
the United States. Presidents serve a term of four
years and, since 1951, may only serve for two terms.

GEORGE
WASHINGTON

ABRAHAM
LINCOLN

FRANKLIN D.
ROOSEVELT

PRESIDENTS OF THE US

STATUE OF
LIBERTY

1789–97	George Washington
1797–1801	John Adams
1801–09	Thomas Jefferson
1809–17	James Madison
1817–25	James Monroe
1825–29	John Quincy Adams
1829–37	Andrew Jackson
1837–41	Martin van Buren
1841	William H. Harrison
1841–45	John Tyler
1845–49	James K. Polk
1849–50	Zachary Taylor
1850–53	Millard Fillmore
1853–57	Franklin Pierce
1857–61	James Buchanan
1861–65	Abraham Lincoln
1865–69	Andrew Johnson
1869–77	Ulysses S. Grant
1877–81	Rutherford B. Hayes
1881	James A. Garfield
1881–85	Chester A. Arthur

1885–89	Grover S. Cleveland
1889–93	Benjamin Harrison
1893–97	Grover S. Cleveland
1897–1901	William McKinley
1901–09	Theodore Roosevelt
1909–13	William H. Taft
1913–21	Woodrow Wilson
1921–23	Warren G. Harding
1923–29	Calvin Coolidge
1929–33	Herbert Hoover
1933–45	Franklin D. Roosevelt
1945–53	Harry S. Truman
1953–61	Dwight D. Eisenhower
1961–63	John F. Kennedy
1963–69	Lyndon B. Johnson
1969–74	Richard Nixon
1974–77	Gerald Ford
1977–81	James Carter
1981–89	Ronald Reagan
1989–93	George Bush
1993–	William J. Clinton

RUSSIAN RULERS

RUSSIAN RULERS have traditionally been known by the title Czar, which means emperor and comes from the Roman title Caesar. In 1917, Russia became part of the Union of Soviet Socialist Republics (USSR), which lasted until 1992.

RUSSIAN MONARCHS

1462–1505	Ivan III, the Great
1505–33	Basil III
1533–84	Ivan IV, the Terrible
1584–98	Fyodor I
1598–1605	Boris Gudunov
1605	Fyodor II
1605–06	Demetrius
1606–10	Basil (IV) Shuiski
1610–13	INTERREGNUM
1613–45	Michael Romanov
1645–76	Alexis
1676–82	Fyodor III
1682–89	Ivan V and Peter I, the Great

CATHERINE THE GREAT

VLADIMIR LENIN

1689–1725	Peter I, the Great
1725–27	Catherine I
1727–30	Peter II
1730–40	Anna
1740–41	Ivan VI
1741–62	Elizabeth
1762	Peter III
1762–96	Catherine II, the Great
1796–1801	Paul I
1801–25	Alexander I
1825–55	Nicholas I
1855–81	Alexander II
1881–94	Alexander III
1894–1917	Nicholas II

KREMLIN CATHEDRAL OF THE ANNUNCIATION

LEADERS OF THE USSR

1917–22	Vladimir Lenin
1922–53	Joseph Stalin
1953–64	Nikita Krushchev
1964–82	Leonid Brezhnev
1982–84	Yuri Andropov
1984–85	Konstantin Chernenko
1985–92	Mikhail Gorbachev
1992–	Boris Yeltsin

RULERS OF FRANCE AND SPAIN

FRENCH MONARCHS and republican leaders are listed from the 10th century onward. Spanish rulers are listed from the 15th century, when Spain was united under Ferdinand and Isabella.

FRENCH MONARCHS

CAROLINGIAN
936–954	Louis IV
954–986	Lothair
986–987	Louis V

CAPET
987–996	Hugh Capet
996–1031	Robert II
1031–60	Henry I
1060–1108	Philip I
1108–37	Louis VI
1137–80	Louis VII
1180–1223	Philip II
1223–26	Louis VIII
1226–70	Louis IX
1270–85	Philip III
1285–1314	Philip IV
1314–16	Louis X
1316	John I
1316–22	Philip V
1322–28	Charles IV

LOUIS XIV

NAPOLEON I

VALOIS
1328–50	Philip VI
1350–64	John II
1364–80	Charles V
1380–1422	Charles VI
1422–61	Charles VII
1461–83	Louis XI
1483–98	Charles VIII
1498–1515	Louis XII
1515–47	Francis I
1547–59	Henry II
1559–60	Francis II
1560–74	Charles IX
1574–89	Henry III

BOURBON
1589–1610	Henry IV
1610–43	Louis XIII
1643–1715	Louis XIV
1715–74	Louis XV
1774–92	Louis XVI

1792–1804	FIRST REPUBLIC

FIRST EMPIRE
1804–14	Napoleon I

BOURBON
1814–24	Louis XVIII
1824–30	Charles X
1830–48	Louis Philippe

1848–52	SECOND REPUBLIC

SECOND EMPIRE
1852–70	Napoleon III

FRENCH PRESIDENTS

THIRD REPUBLIC
1871–73	Adolphe Thiers
1873–79	Patrice de MacMahon
1879–87	Jules Grévy
1887–94	Marie François Sadi Carnot
1894–95	Jean Casimir-Périer
1895–99	François Félix Faure
1899–1906	Émile Loubet
1906–13	Armand Fallières
1913–20	Raymond Poincaré
1920	Paul Deschanel
1920–24	Alexandre Millerand
1924–31	Gaston Doumergue
1931–32	Paul Doumer
1932–40	Albert Lebrun

VICHY GOVERNMENT
1940–44	Henri Philippe Pétain

PROVISIONAL GOVERNMENT
1944–46	Charles de Gaulle
1946	Félix Gouin
1946	Georges Bidault
1946	Léon Blum

FOURTH REPUBLIC
1947–54	Vincent Auriol
1954–59	René Coty

FIFTH REPUBLIC
1959–66	Charles de Gaulle
1969–74	Georges Pompidou
1974–81	Valéry Giscard d'Estaing
1981–1995	François Mitterrand
1995–	Jacques Chirac

SPANISH MONARCHS

1474–1504	Isabella of Castille
1479–1516	Ferdinand II of Aragon

HABSBURG
1516–56	Charles I
1556–98	Philip II
1598–1621	Philip III
1621–65	Philip IV
1665–1700	Charles II

ISABELLA OF CASTILLE

BOURBON
1700–24	Philip V (abdicated)
1724	Louis I
1724–46	Philip V (restored)
1746–59	Ferdinand VI
1759–88	Charles III
1788–1808	Charles IV
1808	Ferdinand VII
1808–13	Joseph Bonaparte
1814–33	Ferdinand VII
1833–68	Isabella II
1870–73	Amadeus of Savoy

1873–74	FIRST REPUBLIC

BOURBON
1874–85	Alfonso XII
1885–86	Maria Cristina (Regent)
1886–1931	Alfonso XIII

1931–39	SECOND REPUBLIC

1939–75	Francisco Franco (Dictator)

BOURBON
1975–	Juan Carlos

PRIME MINISTERS OF THE COMMONWEALTH AND IRELAND

THESE LISTS SHOW the prime ministers of Australia, Ireland, Canada, and New Zealand from the time these countries became independent from Britain.

AUSTRALIAN PRIME MINISTERS

1901–03	Edmund Barton
1903–04	Alfred Deakin
1904	John C. Watson
1904–05	George Houston Reid
1905–08	Alfred Deakin
1908–09	Andrew Fisher
1909–10	Alfred Deakin
1910–13	Andrew Fisher
1913–14	Joseph Cook
1914–15	Andrew Fisher
1915–23	William M. Hughes
1923–29	Stanley M. Bruce
1929–32	James H. Scullin
1932–39	Joseph A. Lyons
1939	Earle Page
1939–41	Robert Gordon Menzies
1941	Arthur William Fadden
1941–45	John J. Curtin
1945	Francis M. Forde
1945–49	Joseph Benedict Chifley
1949–66	Robert Gordon Menzies
1966–67	Harold Edward Holt
1967–68	John McEwen
1968–71	John Grey Gorton
1971–72	William McMahon
1972–75	E. Gough Whitlam
1975–83	J. Malcolm Fraser
1983–91	Robert Hawke
1991–	Paul J. Keating

IRISH PRIME MINISTERS

1922	Arthur Griffith
1922	Michael Collins
1922–32	William Cosgrave
1932–48	Eamonn de Valera
1948–51	John Aloysius Costello
1951–54	Eamonn de Valera
1954–57	John Aloysius Costello
1957–59	Eamonn de Valera
1959–66	Sean Lemass
1966–73	Jack Lynch
1973–77	Liam Cosgrave
1977–79	Jack Lynch
1979–81	Charles Haughey
1981–82	Garrett Fitzgerald
1982	Charles Haughey
1982–87	Garrett Fitzgerald
1987–92	Charles Haughey
1992–94	Albert Reynolds
1994–	John Bruton

CANADIAN PRIME MINISTERS

1867–73	John A. Macdonald	1926–30	W. L. Mackenzie King
1873–78	Alexander Mackenzie	1930–35	Richard Bedford Bennett
1878–91	John A. Macdonald	1935–48	W. L. Mackenzie King
1891–92	John J. C. Abbott	1948–57	Louis St Laurent
1892–94	John Sparrow Thompson	1957–63	John G. Diefenbaker
1894–96	Mackenzie Bowell	1963–68	Lester Bowles Pearson
1896	Charles Tupper	1968–79	Pierre Elliott Trudeau
1896–1911	Wilfred Laurier	1979–80	Charles Joseph Clark
1911–20	Robert Laird Borden	1980–84	Pierre Elliott Trudeau
1920–21	Arthur Meighen	1984	John Napier Turner
1921–26	W. L. Mackenzie King	1984–93	Martin Brian Mulroney
1926	Arthur Meighen	1994	Kim Campbell
		1994–	Jean Chrétien

NEW ZEALAND PRIME MINISTERS

1856	Henry Sewell	1887–91	Harry Albert Atkinson
1856	William Fox	1891–93	John Ballance
1856–61	Edward William Stafford	1893–1906	Richard John Seddon
1861–62	William Fox	1906	William Hall-Jones
1862–63	Alfred Domett	1906–12	Joseph George Ward
1863–64	Frederick Whitaker	1912	Thomas Mackenzie
1864–65	Frederick Aloysius Weld	1912–25	William Ferguson Massey
1865–69	Edward William Stafford	1925	Francis Henry Dillon Bell
1869–72	William Fox	1925–28	Joseph Gordon Coates
1872	Edward William Stafford	1928–30	Joseph George Ward
1872–73	George M. Waterhouse	1930–35	George William Forbes
1873	William Fox	1935–40	Michael J. Savage
1873–75	Julius Vogel	1940–49	Peter Fraser
1875–76	Daniel Pollen	1949–57	Sidney J. Holland
1876	Julius Vogel	1957	Keith J. Holyoake
1876–77	Harry Albert Atkinson	1957–60	Walter Nash
1877–79	George Grey	1960–72	Keith J. Holyoake
1879–82	John Hall	1972	John Marshall
1882–83	Frederick Whitaker	1972–74	Norman Kirk
1883–84	Harry Albert Atkinson	1974–75	Wallace E. Rowling
1884	Robert Stout	1975–84	Robert D. Muldoon
1884	Harry Albert Atkinson	1984–89	David Lange
1884–87	Robert Stout	1989–90	Geoffrey Palmer
		1990	Michael Moore
		1990–	James Bolger

Resources

Museums, libraries, and model villages provide very useful historical resources. Local organizations of this kind will give you information about the area in which you live and should be able to tell you about local history societies and other organizations that offer further information. A small selection of both general and local resources is listed below.

Anchorage Museum of History and Art
W. 7th Ave. and A St.
Anchorage, AK
907/343-6173
Native Alaskan life

Center of Science and Industry
280 E. Broad St.
Columbus, OH
614/228-2674
Street of Yesteryear: late 1800s–early 1900s

Cherokee National Museum
Willis Rd.
Tahlequah, OK
918/456-6007
1500s Cherokee village

Colonial Williamsburg
Williamsburg, VA
804/229-1000
Virginia capital 1699–1780

Colorado History Museum
1300 Broadway
Denver, CO
303/866-3682
Colorado and the West

Computer Museum
300 Congress St.
Cambridge, MA
617/426-2800
Development of machines that calculate and process information

Eunice Museum
220 S.C.C. Duson Rd.
Eunice, LA
318/457-6540
Cajun culture

Heard Museum
22 E. Monte Vista Rd.
Phoenix, AZ
602/252-8840
Native American culture

Henry Ford Museum and Greenfield Village
20900 Oakwood Blvd.
Detroit, MI
313/271-1620
Communications, transportation (including cars), domestic life, agriculture, and industry

Kansas Cosmosphere and Space Center
1100 N. Plum St.
Hutchinson, KS
800/397-0330
Spacecraft; spacesuits

Kansas Museum of History
6425 SW 6th St.
Topeka, KS
913/272-8681
Kansas from Native American era to present

Louisiana State Museum
French Quarter
P.O. Box 2448
New Orleans, LA
504/568-6968
Multicultural history of Louisiana

Museum of American Frontier Culture
230 Frontier Dr.
Staunton, VA
703/332-7850
Early agrarian life

Museum of History and Industry
2700 24th Ave. E
Seattle, WA
206/324-1125
Puget Sound region

Museum of Man
Balboa Park
San Diego, CA
619/239-2001
Anthropology

Museum of Science and Industry
E. 57th St. and
S. Lakeshore Dr.
Chicago, IL
312/684-1414
Model coal mine, spacecraft from early NASA missions; flight simulators

Museum of the City of New York
5th Ave. at 103rd St.
New York, NY
212/534-1672
History of New York City

National Air and Space Museum
The Mall
Washington, DC
202/357-2700
History of aviation

National Museum of American History
The Mall
Washington, DC
202/357-2700
Social, political, and technological history

Patriots Point
US 17
Charleston, VA
803/884-2727
Naval and maritime history

Plimoth Plantation
Rte. 3A, Exit 4
Plymouth, MA
508/746-1622
1627 Pilgrim village

Old Sturbridge Village
1 Old Sturbridge Village Rd.
Sturbridge, MA
508/347-3362
1800s New England town

Stuhr Museum of the Prairie Pioneer
US 34 and US 281
Grand Island, NB
308/385-5316
Native American artifacts; 60-building railroad town

University Museum
33rd and Spruce Sts.
Philadelphia, PA
215/563-3737
Archaeology and anthropology

Western Heritage Museum
801 S. 10th St.
Omaha, NB
402/444-5072
Omaha history 1880–1954

Royal Ontario Museum
100 Queen's Park
Toronto, Ontario, Canada
416/586-5549
Canadian Heritage Floor

Glossary

ABDICATE
(Of a monarch) to give up the throne voluntarily.

ABSOLUTE RULER
A monarch who has complete power over his or her subjects, and is not answerable to a government.

ALLY
A state or person formally united with another, normally by means of a treaty.

ARCHAEOLOGY
The study of the material remains of past human cultures.

ARTIFACT
An object made by a person, such as a tool or a work of art.

BARBARIAN
An uncivilized or primitive person; a member of one of the various peoples who took over after the fall of the Roman Empire.

CITY-STATE
A city with its own independent government.

CIVILIZATION
A complex and well-developed society that usually has large cities, a system of government, an organized religion, and a form of writing.

CIVIL SERVICE
The staff responsible for the administration of a government, such as collection of taxes.

CIVIL WAR
A conflict between groups within one nation or state.

COLONY
Territory that is at some distance from the country that governs it. People from the governing country who live in a colony are called colonists.

CONSTITUTION
An outline of the basic principles by which a nation is governed and the key rights of the citizens.

CULTURE
The ideas, beliefs, and knowledge of a particular people.

DEMOCRACY
Government by the representatives of the people, chosen by free election.

DEPRESSION
An economic slump, generally featuring low investment, high unemployment, and low production levels.

DICTATOR
An absolute and usually tyrannical ruler.

DISCRIMINATION
The singling out of a group for unfair or unfavorable treatment, usually because of race, sex, or membership of a specific minority.

DYNASTY
A group of rulers of the same family.

ECONOMY
The range of activities concerned with producing, selling, and consuming goods and services within a nation.

EMIGRATION
The process of leaving one's native country to settle in another.

EMPIRE
A collection of peoples, areas, or former states under the rule of one person (the emperor).

EPIDEMIC
The widespread occurrence of a disease.

FAMINE
An acute shortage of food.

GOVERNMENT
The way in which a country is ruled; the group of people who rule (govern) a country.

HERETIC
A person who disagrees with some of the beliefs of the local religion. A heretic's beliefs are known as heresy.

HUMAN RIGHTS
The basic rights that a person is entitled to, such as justice and freedom.

INNOVATION
The introduction of something such as a new method or device.

LEGAL SYSTEM
The laws of a country; the system of police, courts, lawyers, and judges who enforce these laws.

LIBERTY
The power of individuals to think, speak, and make choices without unfair government control.

MONARCH
A ruler, usually a king, queen, emperor, or empress.

NATIONALIST
A person who believes in and sometimes fights for the right of an area to become an independent nation.

PARLIAMENT
The national assembly, usually elected democratically, that passes the laws of a country.

POLICY
A system of ideas or plans of a particular country or government.

REFORM
A change in law or policy intended to bring about an improvement.

REGIME
A system of government.

REPUBLIC
A system of government in which the head of the country is elected or nominated.

REVOLUTION
The overthrow of a country's government by a group of its people; an extreme change in the way things are done.

SACRIFICE
Giving up one thing for another, for example giving an offering in return for a god's favor.

SCRIBE
A person who made handwritten copies of documents before the invention of printing.

SERF
A worker in feudal Europe who was not allowed to leave the land he worked on.

SIEGE
A method of warfare involving surrounding a city or castle, cutting off supplies, and attacking.

SOCIETY
A group of peoples with distinctive beliefs, aims, and cultural traditions.

TECHNOLOGY
The practical use of scientific and mechanical skills.

TERRITORY
Land governed by a particular state or ruler.

Index

Acknowledgments

Dorling Kindersley would like to thank:
Hilary Bird for the index; Robin Hunter and Martin Wilson for design assistance; Caroline Potts and John Stevenson for picture research.

Illustrations by:
David Ashby, Peter Bailey, Russell Barnett, Steven Conlin, Peter Dennis (Linda Rogers Associations), Bill Donohoe, Eugene Fleury, Chris Forsey, Luigi Galante, Nick Harris, Nicholas Hewetson, Richard Hook (Linden Artists), Jason Lewis, Angus McBride (Linden Artists), Sergio Momo, Tony Mannis, Tony Morris, Sarah Ponder, Sallie Alane Reason, Sebastian Quigley, Rodney Shackell, Eric Thomas, John Woodcock.

Photographs by:
Peter Anderson, Geoff Brightling, Andy Crawford, Geoff Dann, Philip Dowell, Mike Dunning, David Exton, Chas Howson, Colin Keates, Dave King, Andrew McRobb, Martin Plomer, Tim Ridley, Karl Shone, James Stevenson, Clive Streeter, Michel Zabé.

Picture Credits
t top; *c* center; *b* bottom; *l* left; *r* right.

The publisher would like to thank the following for their kind permission to reproduce their photographs:

Ancient Art & Architecture/Ronald Sheridan 48br, 59tl; Ashmolean Museum, Oxford 1, 2br, 12tr, 25br, 36bl, 37br, 39cl, 41br, 42r, 43cr, tr, 70-71, 82-83c, 87br, 89tc; Bolton Metro Museum 10tr, 35tl; Bridgeman Art Library/Forbes Magazine Collection, New York 120br, Giraudon 60-61b, Kunsthistoriches Museum, Vienna 61cr, Vatican Museums & Galleries 77t; The British Library 44tr; The British Museum 107tl, 123br; Musée de L'Emperi 99tr, tc; The Horniman useum 78l; The Image Bank/Guido Alberto Rossi 139br, Harald Sund 139tr; Imperial War Museum 108bc, 125t, br; Magnum Photos Ltd/Rene Burri: 129c, Marc Riboud: 132cr; Museum of London 11tr, 32tr, bl; Museum of the Moving Image 123cr; National Maritime Museum 3bl, 13br, 35b, 46b; National Museum of Denmark, Copenhagen 10cl, 62tl, 63tr; National Museum of Scotland 76c; National Railway Museum, York 90-91, 105tl; Natural History Museum 21bl; NASA 110-111, 131b; Oslo Ship Museum 62br; Pitt Rivers Museum, Oxford 16-17, 65br, 84tl, 85br; Popperfoto 134c; Range Pictures Ltd/Bettmann 120c, 122b, 124tr, 125bc, 130c, 144l; /UPI 135c; Rex Features Ltd 136; /CTK 134b; /Jacques Witt 133b; Sipa Press 132bc, /Laski 138tr; Robert Wallis 138b; Royal Museum of Scotland 50b; Peter Sanders 136b; Science Museum, London 35b, 96b, 105br, cl, 107br; University Museum of Archaeology & Anthropology, Cambridge 20r, 26-27, 33tl, br, bc, 52-53, 66b; Wallace Collection, London 2tr, 68bl, 81tl, 83tl, 85c, 88tl, cr, 100tl, tr.

Every effort has been made to trace the copyright holders and we apologize in advance for any unintentional omissions. We would be pleased to insert the appropriate acknowledgment in any subsequent edition of this publication.